WHERE THE HELL AM I?

Trips I Have Survived

Ken Levine

March 2011.

For Matt & Annie – may you always have safe and happy travels and call when you get there.

TABLE OF CONTENTS

ACKNOWLEDGMENTS

FIRST OFF, I NEED to thank my family. Their support and sacrifice in letting me take them on lovely vacations was above and beyond the call of duty. I shake my head and often wonder how I got so lucky. But they were always there for me. Whether it was Roy's restaurant in Maui, a Broadway show in New York, or even a Red Sox game at Fenway Park, they hung in there. For me. For my art. There were even times the kids had to miss school for Hawaii. I can never repay them.

But seriously, I am grateful. It's just that acknowledgments are generally so over-the-top. You've written a book, not crossed the Atlantic Ocean in a bathtub!

So with appreciation that hopefully really means something because it's sincere, I salute the following:

Lee Goldberg, Lisa Messinger, Joe Dungan, Blair Richwood, Tom Straw, Alan Eisenstock, and Russ Woody – successful authors and agents who really showed me the ropes. Thanks for sharing your expertise and patiently answering some really stupid questions (like "do I really need acknowledgments?").

Carl Graves for his fabulous cover, and Rob Siders for assembling a jumble of word files into an actual book.

Howard Hoffman for his technical and emotional support.

Jonathan Emerson, Diane Neubauer, and my daughter Annie for going through the manuscript and making me look less illiterate.

Scott Akasaki, the Dodgers' Traveling Secretary who has the thankless task of wrangling twenty-five millionaire ballplayers and still found the time to accommodate me. I don't think there's enough Valium in the world that would allow me to do that job. And I can't mention the Dodgers without thanking the three Joshes – Suchon, Rawitch, and Cumming – for being such great traveling companions.

KABC radio, the Goodspeed Theater, the Seattle Mariners, Harrah's Hotel Las Vegas, the New Mexico Broadcasters Association, the Nashville Film Festival, and HBO funded some of these expeditions. Thanks for the free trips and not making me put out.

Finally, I come full circle and want to properly thank my family. Matt & Annie are the greatest kids a father could ever ask for (you'll see for yourself), and my wife, Debby is nothing short of extraordi-

nary – and that's with me holding down the acknowledgment hyper-
bole. Most of these trips she organized. She was the Levine traveling
secretary, concierge, camp counselor, and in my case – the romantic
leading lady.

INTRODUCTION

IT'S SORT OF THE *Facebook* principle. You collect all these friends, many you haven't actually contacted in months or years, but you connect with them all through your status updates. Before social networks came along I used to keep in touch with my friends via travelogues.

Whenever I went east of Simi Valley I wrote amusing accounts of my adventures and emailed them to the few hundred friends in my address book. (God, that sounds so *primitive!*) And unlike status updates, since I wasn't filing them seven times an hour, I would frequently get replies back, allowing me to stay connected with everyone on my list.

Thus a tradition was born. At first I worried that I wouldn't find enough humorous situations and observations to warrant a full account every trip. I mean, how do you get three pages out of Albuquerque?

But I always found something. Usually more than I needed. Even in Albuquerque. D.H. Lawrence was cremated there and his ashes are mixed in with the cement used to build his burial guesthouse. Seriously, how can seeing that not be on your bucket list?

Absurdity and goofiness and Americana are everywhere (even in Europe). So as long as there are Duck Tours, the "Master Bait & Tackle Shop", Pet Jacuzzis, hotels with voodoo floors, a Cannabis festival, the "Miss Swamp Buggy" beauty contest, 100,000 rubber ducks in the Ohio River, a Minnie Pearl statue, the "Shrub Guy", free dwarf mice, and Hitler's town car on display in a Las Vegas casino there is no shortage of mirth.

And today when you travel, humor is not just a luxury; it's a requirement. Getting anywhere now is an ordeal. Between the TSA, airlines, ground transportation, hotels, and crowds, what once was a leisurely family vacation is now the wire hanger scene in *Mommie Dearest*. So you either laugh or have a psychotic breakdown at the Hertz Gold Club counter.

The travelogues continued. Between vacations, visiting the kids at college, work related sojourns, mounting a musical out of town, and covering major league baseball teams, I've logged thousands of miles from Honolulu to Athens with every Cincinnati and Ft. Lauderdale in between.

When I amassed enough of these reports I considered compiling them into a book. An editor reviewed the material and said he would publish it in a minute... if my name was Dave Barry. But, to use his words, "No one knows who the f*ck you are" "Even with my credits?" I asked. "*M*A*S*H? Cheers? Frasier?*" "Your family is going to buy the book anyway" was his response.

That was six years ago. Today, with my blog, articles in major publications, and radio presence in Los Angeles and Seattle, I can say with complete modesty that I am now well known enough that I can self publish.

So here they are – the highlights and lowlights of 38 of the greatest cities in the U.S. and the world, and 12 average ones. Besides personal experiences there are also travel tips, recommendations, warnings, a little history, and hopefully a few laughs along the way.

You should probably meet my traveling companions. These are the Levines.

My wife Debby is a Brooklyn transplant. She has two masters and a doctorate, as if I wasn't the dumb one in the relationship *already*. Debby's a licensed clinical social worker and the world's greatest mother. She likes art, music, and long walks along the beach even if the ocean is turned off (as it was at the Vegas hotel we once stayed at).

When the book begins my son, Matt is 18 and my daughter, Annie is 14. They're both bright, funny, and already little curmudgeons. Matt eventually went off to Tufts in Boston and is now a design engineer for Apple Computers in Silicon Valley. Annie graduated Northwestern University in Chicago and is well on her way to becoming the next Tina Fey.

When not gallivanting with them I'm usually joined by either my TV/film writing partner, David Isaacs, my *Men Of a Certain Age* industry cronies, or the Los Angeles Dodgers. You'll enjoy traveling with them, too.

Feel free to skip around. Seek out the cities you know and compare your impressions with mine. Or search for destinations you're considering visiting. Or – and I know this is crazy – read the whole book. It's laid out chronologically so there is continuity and variety. But if you just want to read five New York travelogues, be my guest.

When you finish, I invite you to think back to your own trips. Upon reflection, I'll bet there were a lot of funny incidents and encounters that didn't seem amusing at the time. But had you viewed them differently, they might have been. And that's another of my objectives, to get you to approach *your* future vacations with an eye open to the absurd. Trust me, you'll have way more fun...except at O'Hare.

So happy travels. As you'll soon see, mine were. Mostly. In general.

Ken Levine
February 2011

HAWAII

December 2000

WE'RE BACK FROM THE land of cheap fireworks, Don Ho, the Dole factory where pineapple juice comes out of drinking fountains, Zippys take-out, and Japanese tourists. That's right – Hawaii. We had a lovely time, returning like swallows to the Kahala Mandarin Oriental (formerly the Kahala Hilton now the Mandarin ORIENTAL because "Mandarin" just wasn't Oriental enough).

The Kahala Mandarin Oriental Asian has a nickname, which really applies during the Christmas holidays. The KaHollywood Mandarin. Returning regulars like the Jeff Katzenberg family, the Garry Marshall family, and Fiona Apple helped ring in the New Year showbiz style with a party that we weren't invited to.

Cabanas were at a premium and were reserved ahead a time. Someone named Katzenberg. Great tables at breakfast were reserved. Again, that Katzenberg fellow. Lounge chairs were even hard to get. The poolside snack shop still makes the best hotdogs and the little Hawaiian man who prepares them was again getting torn a new asshole by a certain Hollywood producer psycho bitch when he committed the cardinal sin of forgetting to include the tiny plastic cup of cole slaw. Why don't these people love us Hoalies???

We went to Roy's for dinner. As always, exceptional. They're celebrating their 15th anniversary. President Clinton dined there in 1997. He had a food taster (true story). Guess he just likes to surround himself with people who will swallow.

Did not get to the restaurant that featured fried Snickers Bars. The fact that you had to leave your credit card at the door because so many people skipped kind of dissuaded us.

Santa Claus arrived on a long canoe bearing candy canes for the kids. He was clad only in a traditional cap and red skirt. The children were confused. Not like any Santa they had ever seen. What I didn't realize until that day was how many tattoos Santa had. Or how scary his heavily-tattooed Samoan elf was.

Friday's activities included a nose flute demonstration. I believe that's the same instrument Neil Young has snorted for thirty years.

Spam is on sale for $1.29 a can. And that actually gets these people into a store

Matt got stung by a bee. The pool staff sprung into action. Nothing gets out bee venom like Evian Mist.

How do they make Dippin' Dots?

Annie received a fortune that said, "Seek professional help."

Got in an elevator as a woman was pushing the button. She wore a baseball cap with an "L" on it. I asked what the L stood for and she said, "Lobby." Do I really look THAT stupid??

"Mahalo" means thank you. But I understand that since it's written on every trash can many tourists think "mahalo" means "trash."

Went snorkeling. Found Nemo. Went to Roy's. Ate Nemo.

Debby needed emergency dental work and Matt came down with some mystery island poison ivy type rash. This trip is beginning to sound like *Hello Muddah, Hello Faddah*. Both are fine thanks to drugs, pain killers, antibiotics, ice packs, salves, ointments, steroids, and numbing swabs (fortunately, items that every Jew normally carries).

Tia Carrere is now singing at a Waikiki hotel. This is my favorite Tia Carrere quote: "I love to sing, so I just figured that I was going to sing or something."

There's now a bronze bust of Jack Lord at the Kahala Mall. Considering all the work he had done to his face the bust could actually *be* Jack Lord.

The highlight of the trip was the kids being able to swim with the two dolphins that are in the Kahala Mandarin Oriental Far Eastern lagoon. The third dolphin was in Mr. Katzenberg's bathtub I believe.

And as I return to real life (kicking and screaming) I leave you with this:

Aia a pa'i'io ka maka, ha'i'ia kupuna nana 'oe.

(Only when your face is slapped should you tell who your ancestors are.)

Aloha.

NEW YORK

May 2000

GOLDIE HAWN WAS ON our flight. The pressurized cabin really does wonders for all her face work.

Stayed at the Omni Berkshire on 52nd Street. Nice hotel. One complaint: their pay-per-view movies were all actual Hollywood movies. Yeah, that's what businessmen alone in their rooms want to see – Martin Lawrence comedies. To me, a trip to New York City isn't complete without checking in on the latest adventures of that housewife who always seems to be home alone and that nice Jehovah's Witness who looks like Ron Jeremy.

Visited relatives in Forest Hills. Prices for homes out there are on a par with Beverly Hills. It's outrageous. Especially since two blocks away it looks like the neighborhood from every Spike Lee film.

On Sunday in Manhattan they had an Israeli Parade, a Cuban Parade, and a bike race. Thereby insuring that every single street was blocked off and no one could get into the city to participate or view any of them.

Spectacular weather the entire trip. Even the Carole King-looking girls (60% of the N.Y. female population) shed their customary schlump coats.

My favorite store was no longer in operation. The guy with the card table on Broadway selling "Cool As Shit Jewelry." Hopefully, he's now on QVC. "Yo, bitches! Time to update your bling!"

Check the *Playbill* of any Broadway show. Every single cast member has appeared in *Law & Order*.

It's May and the Mets are already hurting. They have radio ads promoting their upcoming series with the Houston Astros…in August.

Finally, a trip down to Ground Zero. It is so profound and deeply moving. And yet, I saw people taking it in as if were just another tour attraction in Fun City. ("After Ground Zero, maybe we can find the apartment building from *Friends*.") I still can't fathom the event itself, and being there, seeing it in person, makes it even harder to believe. Guess we all have to deal with it in our own way. What helped me today was going up to every fireman and policeman I saw and just thanking them.

Some closing observations: everyone smokes, everyone has a cell phone (which makes it harder to tell who the crazy people are since everyone seems to be talking to themselves), and there are an awful lot of very pregnant women. My guess is most of them have the same due date. June 11th.

BOSTON

October 2002

DOES IT ALWAYS RAIN and drizzle in Boston? It did for the four days I was there.

Matt is doing swell at Tufts, and it was great to spend a fortune feeding him this weekend. We were there for parents' weekend, but didn't read the calendar very well. Parents' weekend is next weekend. Lucky we didn't show up at the president's house for that Sunday morning breakfast.

First up was Legal Seafood on Thursday night, where Matt and I went with my radio friend, Dale Dorman. He's been a fixture in Boston radio for over 30 years and clearly is considered a god. The restaurant was packed, he said his name, and we were shown a table within an hour.

I had lobster.

Debby and Annie came in on the redeye Friday morning and immediately wanted to go outlet shopping. We don't have a Gap outlet in California? I decided not to go, preferring to do, well…ANYTHING else. So I spent the day with Dale at KISS 108.

They have a great contest. Four people are living inside a Mini Cooper. The last person to leave gets to keep the car. Two guys and two girls. The girls bolted almost immediately (proving that women *are* smarter than men). So to keep the remaining flood victims company, the station threw a big dog in the car. It's on display at Faneuil Hall so sleeping is impossible because all these homeless guys knock on the windows all night. This for a twelve thousand dollar automobile that will probably have to be boiled to get the stench out.

Sirens in Boston are goofy. No wonder people drive like raving maniacs there. They have the police force from Toontown.

Tourists still flock to bar that served as the model for *Cheers*. It's the place to go if you want to see real people from Louisville or Gainesville. "Hey, this don't look nothing like the bar we see on the magic picture box." No, that's because it wasn't FILMED there. Norm, Cliff, Sam, and Diane DON'T EXIST. Befuddled, these tourists eat their overpriced lunches, buy sweatshirts, mugs, and other outrageously costly souvenirs and head off to the Freedom Trail where they could purchase New England Patriots jerseys actually signed by George Washington and Paul Revere.

Tufts University is very pretty. It is in Medford, which is not. Actual store sign: "LIVE POULTRY: FRESHLY KILLED."

Saw Matt's apartment. It's a former S.L.A. hideout.

Toured Matt's frat house. Picture any structure in Kansas after being hit full force by a twister.

The leaves haven't really turned yet. Except in the Mini Cooper.

Taxis in Boston are interesting. They have two fare options. Either "when you're not in a hurry," or for $3.00 more "they'll rush." Every cab I took had at least one warning light flashing on its dashboard. My first cabbie plowed into a car, sheepishly saying to me "I didn't see him." Didn't SEE him? It was a Windstar right in front of you on a one-lane street in Harvard Square.

Ever notice that when you go to another city you can never find a radio station you like, but every time you climb into a taxi the driver is listening to a station in his native foreign language? I was treated to twenty minutes of a Haitian station on one cab ride. The Classic Hits station has to change formats because it had no listeners yet there's a Haitian station…and not just any Haitian station – a Haitian TALK station…in BOSTON.

Sunday we had brunch at the Charles hotel. (Get the idea that all we did was eat?) Big celebrity sighting: Natalie Portman. She's one of my son's faves. I offered to lend him my *Becker* fleece, figuring that would really make her swoon, but he passed. Annie saw her across the room and mumbled, "Sweetie, you're making a kazillion dollars a movie – that is the ugliest sweater I have ever seen in my life!" My charming daughter also said, earlier when we were all talking about the new shows and specifically *Good Morning Miami*, "Oh yeah…more washed up people that Dad worked with."

We were late leaving Boston. They had to take one piece of luggage off the flight. So they sent for a baggage handler, he had some accident, they had to send for an ambulance, and then get a second baggage handler. Thus the answer to the question: How many American Airlines employees does it take to remove one suitcase? Six.

Latest update: the dog can't stand the stench and has left the Mini Cooper. But Joe and Miles are still there.

ALBUQUERQUE

June 2003

ALBUQUERQUE IS THE LAND of enchantment where you can buy turquoise jewelry in any 7-11. Spent the weekend speaking at the New Mexico Broadcasters Association's annual convention. Was hoping to get to the D.H. Lawrence burial site, but alas time did not permit. Apparently he was cremated and mixed in the cement used to build the annex off the main ranch house. So you can actually be "inside" D.H. I'm sure when Jackie Collins goes she's going to do the same thing (for the four people who haven't had that privilege already).

I did manage to see the new stadium for the Albuquerque Isotopes, their AAA farm club. My writing partner, David, and I coined the team name "Isotopes" for a *Simpsons* episode we wrote, and the Albuquerque ballclub adopted it. The city is divided. Half thinks it's great (to them I say, "You're welcome") and the other half finds it ridiculous (Hey, we wrote it as a JOKE). Anyway, I was disappointed that the "Topes" were out of town. Was kinda hoping they'd honor me at a game and let me throw out the first drunk.

Stayed at the Marriott, site of the convention. Prime location. Walking distance to a Bennigans, TGI Fridays, Buca de Beppa, and a mall with TWO Dillard department stores. Don't tell someone you'll meet them in front of Dillards because it could cause mass confusion.

Went to the big Friday night reception. Entertainment provided by an Army band. Picture seven silver-haired gentlemen in dress uniforms playing Santana tunes. Oddly, when it came time to present the colors and do the National Anthem a tape was played. Huh??? They don't trust an Army band to do the Star Spangled Banner, but it's okay for them to mangle "Smooth?"

The freeway near our hotel was closed off. There was a jumper. I had no idea just how distraught people were over this Isotope name thing.

Albuquerque is the only city I've ever been to where there's a bowling alley across the street from another bowling alley. Of course

I shouldn't be surprised when there are two Dillard's in one mall. A group of us went to the Leisure Bowl where we hit their karaoke bar at about 10:00. Maybe it was all the drinks I had at the reception but I got talked into going up there to sing.

Guess what? I was terrible.

And just a tad self-conscious. Looking out at all the cowboy hats and bouffant hair, I don't think I ever felt more Jewish. As far as they were concerned, I might as well have sung "Shalom Alechem." Instead I tried to do Neil Sedaka's classic "Breaking Up Is Hard To Do" thinking it was the slow bluesy version. No, it was the bouncy 1962 bubblegum version.

In a desperate attempt to save myself I began talking through the bridge, announcing, "Hey, time to sign up for the summer leagues!" and "two for one bowling for the next fifteen minutes!" When I finished, thinking of becoming the second jumper of the night, a drunk girl from the next table leaned over and slurred, "You was fuckin' GREAT!" She followed that by saying, "I've been here since five!"

At the big awards banquet the next night, I sat at a table with a gentleman from Waco, Texas who proudly announced that his town was the last to lynch a man. "Check!!!"

Heading home today, I was selected for a full security search at the Albuquerque airport. Again, I'm thinking they've never seen a person of the Hebraic persuasion before. The kid with the Mohawk, pierced eyebrow and nose, and Columbine coat whistled right through, but the schmuck in a Polo shirt needed to be body searched.

A fun trip nonetheless. Special thanks to Sparky, Paula, Pam, Duffy, Rooney, and that tragic lush who liked my singing.

BOSTON

October 2003

ANOTHER TRIP TO BOSTON to visit Matt. The town was in mourning because the Red Sox had just lost the American League pennant to the hated Yankees. Everyone wants to kill Sox manager, Grady Little. And considering the way these people drive, that's not an idle threat.

The local newspapers were oh so kind and forgiving. One showed a picture of him with the caption: "Jessica Simpson could manage this team better."

Even the gala annual "Head of the Charles" rowing competition did little to ease the locals' pain. Hundreds of rowing crews compete down the Charles while seven people watch from the riverbanks. It's quite a spectacle. My favorite team, Frankfurter Rudergesellschaft Germania, got their butts kicked by the Garda Siochana Boat Club. I say check the oars for cork!

A number of these teams were staying at my hotel. They weren't hard to spot. Men and women with Popeye arms. Many flew from great distances. But so what? These are the only people who actually feel there's enough legroom in coach.

Swung by the Quincy Market. There we ran across the new second *Cheers* bar. This one, they claim, is set up exactly like the one on TV. Maybe if you've never seen the show. The bar is square and two or three of the pictures on the back wall are the same. Otherwise, the bar on *Star Trek: Deep Space Nine* looks more like the real *Cheers*. A life-size poster of Shelley Long beckons diners to stop by the gift shop before they leave. And there they can purchase *Cheers* ANYTHING. A can of "Norm Nuts." A water bottle for twelve bucks. T-shirts and sweatshirts galore. *Cheers* Bloody Mary mix. *Cheers* underwear. I asked if they had Sam Malone condoms and they didn't get the joke. Nor did they laugh when I inquired about Diane Chambers Xanex.

There are way more men than women who sport pony tails in Boston.

Spotted at the Harvard Yard Pizzeria Uno – A big banner that read:

"Now Serving Breakfast," with two Samuel Adams logos on either side of it.

Blue Laws still exist in Massachusetts. Hand holding between couples is not allowed on Sunday. And for the longest time, liquor stores were not open on Sunday...EXCEPT for one – Super Bowl Sunday (true story). Now they better stay open... at least through the World Series.

SANTA BARBARA

July 2003

WITH BOTH KIDS AWAY this summer (I forget where) my wife and I snuck off to Santa Barbara for a long weekend. Other than the speeding ticket and dropping my cell phone in a pool it was a wonderful trip. Santa Barbara has become the land of the "smart writers who got out and bought when prices were still affordable." Now one must go to Lodi.

Every structure in Santa Barbara is made of stucco. Every floor is tiled. Every hotel room has pictures of the mission. Maybe one in a gazillion tourists come up to Santa Barbara to see the friggin' mission.

Shacks are referred to as "cottages."

Golden Girls writers have gorgeous homes up there. But I'm not bitter.

We stayed at the Inn at the Spanish Gardens. Lovely hotel. Not as nice as Bob Zemickis' tool shed but still. Walking distance to State Street and in a perfect location: down the block from the Council of Drug Prevention and Alcoholism. Across the street from Legal Services. And around the corner from the Probation Department. It was the Ritz-Carlton of Watts.

The town was jumping. All the guys looked like Ashton Kutcher or Jerry Garcia. All the women looked like Demi Moore or Ashton Kutcher.

Sue Grafton, the mystery author, lives up in Santa Barbara. And so, in following her lead...

S is for Sushi – There are sushi restaurants on every block. Typical small town America.

I is for Informercial – My favorite store in Santa Barbara is called "As Seen on TV." It offers all the dandy items you see on television that you order by phone. From Vegematics to that miracle foam thing you put between your knees when you're sleeping, they have it all. My favorite is the Jane Fonda treadmill with the great added feature that there's nothing to plug in! It uses no electricity. You generate the belt moving by yourself! Excuse me, but isn't that called "walking"??? You're paying $200 to walk??? Shouldn't it be called the "Jane Fonda Hamster Wheel?" I overheard a customer say "How does this place stay in business if you can return stuff because none of this crap actually works?"

O is for the Oxiclean kit we bought. I never have to pour or measure detergent again! How did I live without this?

W is for the Wizard Pancake maker (which also makes donuts at no extra cost).

R is for Rain – It rained Saturday. First time in late July in Santa Barbara since the Cenozoic Era. But did real estate values go down?? Nooooo.

A is for Appalled – When I called the front desk and reserved an in-room massage, I gave my name as Kobe Bryant. (Note: at the time he was charged with raping a girl in his hotel room.)

P is for Politically Incorrect – Santa Barbara boasts the first (and now only) Sambo's restaurant. Noted without comment… except…come on guys!

E is for End of an Era – the mask store on State Street is going out of business. Where will people who eat at Sambo's get their masks?

H is for Heist – I saw an officer of the SBPD tooling around on a motorized scooter. If you want to rob a bank and your getaway vehicle is anything but a Segway I'd seriously consider Santa Barbara.

G is for Great Food – The Palace Grill and Andersons.

M is for Mission – Okay, we went to a mission after all. Gorgeous, impressive, truly majestic. No wait, that was our friends, Dave & Sally's new house in Ojai.

N is for Nude Beaches – they have them in Santa Barbara. Considering that most people I saw shouldn't wear shorts much less go naked, I did not visit.

Z is for Zorro – who, as legend has it, bought his first mask at the mask store on State Street.

CHICAGO

August 2003

BACK FROM ONE OF my favorite places – *Chi Town, My Town, the Big Shoulders, the Windy City, the Hog Butcher to the World.* Chicago is truly glorious the three months there's no wind chill factor.

Debby and I went back to collect Annie who had been at Northwestern University for a five-week intensive theatre program for high school kids.

Stayed at the Doubletree Suites (Holiday Inn with cookies). They have the following sign hanging on the towel rack in the bathroom

WHEN YOU CARE, IT SHOWS
"Dear Guest,
Everyday millions of gallons of water are used to wash towels that have only been used once. YOU MAKE THE CHOICE:
A towel on the rack means "I will use again."
A towel on the floor means "Please replace"
Thank you for helping us conserve the Earth's vital resources.

How many housekeeping people were they able to lay-off as a result? How many trees were cut down to make those little signs?

I'm just glad that little announcement wasn't on the toilet paper.

In the honor bar Sparkling Water cost $2.75. At that price they'll never run out of it. They care and it shows.

Dinner Thursday night at Hugo's Frogbar (Gibson's sister restaurant). Nothing like a Chicago steak. Best animal fat in America. Rush Street is quite the happening scene on a warm summer night. Packed with people drinking. Since valet parking is $9.00, I suspect none of them had cars so they all got home safely. The care continues to show.

Anytime you turn on Channel 7, Oprah is on.

My wife forgot to bring perfume so everyday she would duck into Marshall Fields or Bloomingdales and get a free spritz. Meanwhile, I would sneak into the Apple Store and check my email. Who says traveling is expensive?

The big thing in Chicago these days is "Caramel Crisp." This is caramel covered popcorn and the shop that sells it on Michigan Avenue has LINES. Considering the beef, deep dish pizza, pancakes, White Castle sliders, etc. that Chicagoans devour, this must be considered eating light.

There is no greater place in the world to watch a baseball game than Wrigley Field. Nowhere even close. We went Friday afternoon. Cubs vs. Arizona (that classic rivalry). The game started at 2:20. By 3:20 they were beginning the fifth inning. The game ended at 10:05 (But more on that later). Picked up a Harry Caray bobblehead doll. Outside of Wrigley Field they have a statue of Harry Caray, their long-time announcer. On Michigan Avenue they have a statue of another sportscaster, Jack Brickhouse. You have to love a town that erects statues for baseball announcers. Here in LA. the best they can do for Vin Scully is a star on the Hollywood *Walk of Fame*, which is lovely until you realize there's also one for Bugs Bunny, Trigger, and Charlie Tuna.

Across the street from Wrigley is a stand that sells "Sunglasses and Tattoos."

Everyone sitting around us was plastered. We got a foul ball in our section that went off six hands before landing in the lap of the old lady wearing an Ozzie Osbourne T-shirt. Don't drink and catch.

At 4:15 the rains came, delaying the game. Debby and I had to leave anyway, agreeing to meet Annie for dinner in Evanston at 5:00. It rained hard for three hours. I just kept wondering how many towels you could wash as a result. The Cubs and Diamondbacks resumed playing and would continue through 14 innings. We bar hopped along Rush watching the game, cursing the futile Cubs like everyone else.

The Cubbies finally won in only 7 hours, 40 minutes. A day/night single-header. A thousand people were left in the stands. Every one needed a designated driver.

I saw the apartment building they used for *The Bob Newhart Show*. Bet I was the only person in fifteen years to recognize it.

There is a Pancake House for every three Chicagoans.

Gino's Pizza and Shaw's Crab House were as delicious and fattening as ever. But the best meal we had was at Roy's. No one does "corn fed" better than those Hawaiians.

In honor of the upcoming Elvis festival, the WGN morning weather idiot AND the anchor, donned Elvis costumes. The anchor actually read a few stories wearing that getup. How about being Edward R. Murrow impersonators and report the news?

Sunday afternoon produced the worst local flooding in 45 years. You could even wash bed sheets everyday with that much water! People were diving into theatres to get out of the rain...except for those theatres showing *Gigli*. It was still preferable to be pelted with hail.

Coming home, Annie was detained by airport security at O'Hare because of her teddy bear. Excuse me, but isn't that racial profiling? They then searched through her backpack and let her go through, even with a pair of scissors. Huh???

One traveler was unclear that when he had to put his shoes in the plastic bin to go through the X-ray machine, he had to take them off first.

Time to unpack and not wash any of our dirty clothes. Because of course, we *care*.

LAS VEGAS

March 2004

MARCH MADNESS HAS ARRIVED again – the NCAA basketball tournament. Thus the sacred pilgrimage to Las Vegas for me and three of my middle-aged sports nerd television executive buddies. Slater, the Banger, and Mr. Syracuse. Slater brought his girlfriend (who goes by either Karen or Valerie – long story) thus increasing his chances of "getting lucky" by maybe 1%. Mr. Syracuse brought his wife, thus decreasing his chances. My son, Matt flew in from Boston. He's now 21 so what better way to see Las Vegas for the first time than with his dad and three guys who look like the Pep Boys?

We stayed this year at the Paris Hotel. The theme is French hospitality (an oxymoron). I'm sure I would have been given a nicer room if I registered as Himmler. The casino features a low ceiling that is painted to look like the sky, a la the Pirates of the Caribbean ride at Disneyland. It's an odd shade of blue however, one that suggests nuclear winter. There are cobblestone streets and carpeting. A replica LePont Alendre III bridge overlooks the nickel slot machines, and there is an Eiffel Tower that is fifty stories high. Tours are offered. There is a sign at the entrance that reads "No food, beverages, smoking, weddings (true story)".

Matt and I went to Le Cafe for breakfast. They said "inside or outside?" What??? Outside of course meant under the sky-painted ceiling. We chanced it that it wouldn't rain and took the outside.

The in-house cable had a channel that spelled out emergency exit procedures. Leave it to the French to provide a surrender strategy.

This stunned me: The Mirage features "Siegfried & Roy's Secret Garden & Dolphin Habitat." The ad says: "come face to face with Royal White Tigers." How drunk do you have to be or how much money do you have to lose to want to do THAT???

One thing you can say about Vegas, it has the most amazingly beautiful women in the world. And so where did we spend 90% of our time? At the sports book, the one place that none of them would ever be caught dead in. There were 48 games in four days. At times four were going on simultaneously. I'm betting on teams I've never heard of. The place was packed with rowdy men and good old boys chugging long neck beers. We ordered White Russians, Tequila Sunrises, and Rusty Nails. No one messed with US.

One hazard: You see the same commercial seventeen thousand times. Especially the one for "Cialis," designed to keep a man *ready* for 36 hours. Too bad I'm not single. One of those magic pills would be perfect for me. 35 1/2 hours to find a woman then a half hour to perform.

Interesting that it is politically incorrect for colleges to have team names of Indians but it's okay to have the North Carolina Tar Heels and the Manhattan Jaspers.

In keeping with the theme, French accordion music came out of the urinals. Finally, an appropriate venue for that music.

Elegant dining = no Keno boards.

Saturday night at the MGM Grand in Las Vegas at 8:30 I saw a beautiful bride. Long white gown, the veil – she was lovely. And up about a hundred up at the blackjack table!

Slater's girlfriend Valerie/Karen is a vegan, which means there are only six things she can eat and she's allergic to four of them. She and Slater are the two nicest people on the planet but I have dubbed them "America's Waiter Killer Couple." Slater switches every table and sends back every order while Valerie/Karen has the kitchen prepare items not on the menu. I would give anything to see these two on *Survivor*.

Spotted at the Paris pool – a guy toting a ball and chain. I'm guessing (hoping) it was a bachelor party, but there he was with a bowling ball attached to a chain handcuffed to his arm. Either that or the hotel was presenting *Les Miserables* poolside.

What is Pai Gow poker???

McCarran airport always has this wonderful feature – recordings of stars telling you to use the people movers. I remember once hearing Totie Fields a week after her leg was amputated.

At the end of the weekend all of us either made a little money or broke even, Weber State got eliminated, and the waiters at the Paris hotel got together and paid for Slater's cab to the airport.

It was great great fun. Go Jaspers!!!

PALM SPRINGS

December 2004

THE LEVINES DECIDED ON a more abbreviated trip this holiday season. A long weekend in Palm Springs. Turns out it was just like Hawaii. All those beautiful sandy beaches…but a much farther walk to the ocean.

We drove down on Christmas Eve. It was my first time on the Sonny Bono Memorial Freeway. Not surprisingly, it was not tree lined.

Passed the new Morongo casino. Matt found it amusing that a casino would have "*moron*" in its name.

The two big things to do in Palm Springs are play golf or let Sinatra get you laid. So now there's only one thing.

Easy to tell the locals. The men wear red polyester pants with white belts and the women dye their hair the color of Huckleberry Hound.

We stayed at a small resort called 7 Springs. We made the reservations on the ORBITZ website. No wonder we got such a good deal. The hotel knew nothing of our reservations. Even with a confirmation number. That number simply confirms that ORBITZ has successfully cashed your deposit. Fortunately they had accommodations, but the rooms would only be available in three hours. Why so late? The Christmas Party. Housekeeping is shut down until gift exchange. The 7 Springs is a far cry from the 4 Seasons.

And we learned (only upon arrival) that they take pets. And not just little pets. BIG angry pets. Pets that are not used to being cooped up in hotel rooms. Pets that don't like the idea of my wife using the pool. Matt suggested all guests be issued a tranquilizer gun at check-in.

Since we had three hours to kill while housekeeping exchanged stolen bath towels we took a stroll down the main drag, Palm Canyon Boulevard. This is the Waikiki of Palm Springs. T-shirt shops, tank shirt shops, wife-beater shirt shops. Like Hollywood Boulevard they have their own "*walk of fame*" with stars in the sidewalk honoring various Palm Springs celebrities. Stars included Liberace (of course), Sandler & Young, Elke Sommer, Rich Little, Kay Ballard, Victoria Principal, Nancy Sinatra (the only female star who *didn't* sleep with Sinatra), "Iron Eyes" Cody, cowboy rope trickster Montie Montana (who once performed at my elementary school), and Cheetah "the Chimp" (no foolin') listed as *star of stage, film, TV.* Appropriately, his star was right next to Chevy Chase's. For those who don't remember, Cheetah was Tarzan's sidekick in many films and had a brief affair with Maureen O'Sullivan. One star they featured that does not have a corresponding one on Hollywood Boulevard is "Borko B. Djordjevic, M.D.-*Plastic Surgeon/Humanitarian.*" Annie quipped: "Boy, people must've been really ugly to have made him a *humanitarian.*"

Like Sinatra, Bob Hope, and President Eisenhower, Cheetah had a compound out here. Actually he's still there. At 71, Cheetah is the oldest living chimp in captivity. I bet he looks great in red pants with a white belt and still pines for Maureen O'Sullivan.

In Hawaii a big problem is always trying to find a restaurant open on Christmas Eve. No such worries in Palm Springs. I guess because they get JEWS here, but we had no problem getting into the LG steakhouse on Palm Canyon, conveniently located near the "Crazy Shirt" emporium. On Christmas night we hit the "Great Wall" Chinese restaurant and saw the same customers we saw the night before at the LG steakhouse and earlier that day at Sherman's Deli.

Surprisingly, Sherman's is quite good. It has to be judging by the autographed celebrity pictures proudly displayed. Kay Ballard, Keely Smith, and Sandler & Young. I guess Cheetah thought his blintzes were undercooked.

Going through the local paper I noticed there were more ads for dermatologists than "after Christmas sales."

There is a Trump 29 casino nearby. Who knew Donald Trump was an Indian?

Jacuzzi capacity at the 7 Springs: eight people, six pets.

I wonder if Sinatra ever got Cheetah laid.

The Art Museum featured selections from the William Holden collection. Probably empty whiskey bottles from around the world.

There are 15 Thai restaurants on Palm Canyon Dr. Why??? Considering the mean age of the local population is 106, I can't imagine there's that much demand.

The first two days were clear and cold (But a "dry" cold). On Sunday Debby and Annie invaded the outlets at Cabazon (a stunt they wouldn't even subject contestants to on *Fear Factor*). Matt and I checked out the Spa Casino. It made me long for the Debbie Reynolds hotel and casino in Laughlin, Nevada. (I always imagine Debbie getting an urgent page, "Come quick, Ms. Reynolds, the toilet in 604 is overflowing. Bring a plunger!") A Palm Springs casino means 90% slot machines, maybe fifteen gaming tables, no craps, no sports book, video roulette, and aisles wide enough for walkers. But at least no pets!

All foibles aside, it was great for the family to get together even for a few days. (Damn these kids for having their own lives!) Next year Hawaii or the Debbie Reynolds hotel in Laughlin, it really doesn't matter.

Happy New Year. May 2005 be for you what 2004 was for the Boston Red Sox...and 1945 was for Cheetah (the year he and Maureen O'Sullivan took the aerial tramway to the moon).

CHICAGO

January 2005

LAX IS NOW EVEN more impossible, crowded, and confusing. I took my shoes off only to find myself in the Starbucks line. Security checkpoints now have little drawings of what you can't take on a plane. They show a gun, a knife, and my favorite – a round bomb with a fuse ala the Road Runner. Yeah, that's what terrorists are using these days – ACME explosives.

I went to Chicago to visit Annie at Northwestern for the weekend. The dead of winter is always the toughest time for a freshman, so I thought a little care package from home that included free meals was just the ticket. Besides, I miss her.

Southwest Airlines has the longest security lines in history. It's like waiting for the Pirates of the Caribbean except that after an hour, instead of going on a ride you get to watch the girl in front of you put her diaphragm case in the plastic bin for all to see.

You know you're in trouble when the lead story on a local Chicago newscast is the weather. But at least the newscasters weren't dressed like Elvis. The highest temperature for the entire weekend was 12 degrees. Mostly it was 3 degrees with a wind chill factor of -3. As someone who wears a sweater in August in Tucson, this was a bit of a shock to me. As the expression goes: It was colder than Ann Coulter's tit.

Preparation for the cold: I bought this new space age sheer "Body Armor" long underwear. It's kind of like spandex. I've been giving serious thought to becoming a superhero lately and now I have a great head start on my supersuit. I looked like Mr. Incredible after he decided to come out of retirement.

All the leaves are brown. And the sky is gray. Chicago has had a grand total of eleven minutes of sun this month.

Stayed at the Orrington Hotel in Evanston. Everyone there was very nice. This always unnerves me. I don't understand Chicago. They have the worst weather, worst traffic, the Bears, and an average cholesterol of 300. Makes you wonder just what they put in those deep dish pizzas.

Forget Animal Rights Groups. There were TV commercials for "Adriana's Furs." Mink coats, beaver coats – sale prices, come and get 'em! This is not a city intimidated by Bob Barker.

On one of the bulletin boards in Annie's dorm there was a flier on how to "Deal with Depression." It referred to "Seasonal Affective Disorder" or SAD (I always wondered how they came up with that word). They didn't report the cure however, which is "Finally Leaving Oppressive Rotten Icy Deepfreeze Area" or FLORIDA.

NASHVILLE

May 2005

YEEE HAW! JUST BACK from attending the Nashville Film Festival, which, as luck would have it, was held in Nashville this year. My writing partner, David Isaacs, and I were asked to speak on a panel along with fellow schtickmeister, Peter Casey (one of the creators of *Frasier*). Peter's wife, Rosie, joined us. She's a very talented singer/songwriter who comes to Music City U.S.A. often and has the town wired. The only thing she couldn't seem to find was the Country Music Hall of Fame and Museum.

You can't swing a dead Nashville cat in this town without hitting a church. It is the only city in the world with more churches than Starbucks.

Nashville is the home of country music and Jack Daniel's. This is not a coincidence.

People here are quick to point out there is a big difference between country music and country/western music. Country song: "I Can Never Make You Love Me." Country/western song: "How Can I Kiss the Lips at Night that Chewed My Ass All Day Long?"

Didn't visit Dollywood, Conway Twitty City, Opryland, or the Willie Nelson Museum. I just didn't have that extra hour.

Oprah was raised in Nashville. So was Tim McCarver. Thank God for Jack Daniel's.

On Friday we did our panel called "Face the Music." Gifted songwriters wrote spec TV theme songs and we were to critique them. Three idiots who knew nothing about music. We'd babble on about how this or that didn't work, was too retro, not original enough, etc. Then the composers would stand. They all looked like ZZ Top frontmen. You never heard such backtracking. "But it's a great song. I loved it! You have a definite hit here!" I slept that night with the light on.

There is a statue in town of Minnie Pearl.

Minnie Pearl is to Music City what Kitty Carlisle is to Manhattan. The homes all look like Tara and each is rich in history. One of the songwriters I met said thousands of confederate soldiers died in his backyard. That's the kind of thing you insist the previous owners remove.

The town motto: "All you need is three chords and the truth."

Friday night, we were subjected to a screenplay reading. I longed to be one of those confederate soldiers. It was an alleged taut sci-fi thriller performed by local thespians. The lead character was supposed to be the preeminent authority on quantum physics. He was played by Billy Ray Cyrus (I kid you not). I'm only sorry his Nobel Prize winning colleague wasn't played by Junior Samples.

We strolled down Broadway and soaked up all the great honky tonk vibes. Ducked into "Ernest Tubb's Records" and found an album any serious collector would kill for: *William Bendix sings and tells Pirate Stories*. There he was on the cover in a pirate's costume with a peg leg. Arrrgggg!

No one knows the difference between the CMA and the ACM. And they both have annual award shows every month.

The Jack Daniel's distillery in nearby Lynchburg offers free tours. As you drive out you notice that all the people driving back are weaving in and out of lanes and going at 100 m.p.h.

Tried to have breakfast at the famous Pancake Pantry, but there was an hour wait. It's not like they were serving Komodo Dragon. Who waits an hour for friggin' pancakes???

Finally did get to the Country Music Hall of Fame. It was pretty spectacular even if you're not a Homer & Jethro fan. (I, of course, am.) Among the exhibits is a video of Billy Ray Cyrus being interviewed. I turned to David and said, *"There he is on Inside the Actors Studio."* If you see one thing in Nashville make it the CMHOF.

While checking out we noticed that the gentleman at the front desk looked just like Bob Newhart. Later, at the Nashville airport, we heard a page for "Robert Hartley." And, (I swear this is true) five minutes later Marcia Wallace walked in. (She played Carol on the *Bob Newhart Show*). She was in town hawking her book. Marcia's a dear old friend and one of the funniest ladies I know. When her son announced he wanted to become an actor she said "Fine. Act like you *like* me."

See you at the CMA awards…Or is it the ACM awards?

LONDON

May 2005

DAVID AND I ARE very excited about the new pilot we're writing for two reasons. 1) It will star the brilliant actor-comedian, Omid Djalili, and 2) (even more important) we got a free trip to London to go over the script with him. Omid is British-Iranian (he was a regular on the *Whoopi* NBC sitcom last year, which explains why you've never seen or heard of him). It's a little early in the season to be writing a pilot but we wanted the script in before our country attacked Iran.

Flew first class on United. You sit in these big Captain Kirk chairs as if you're on the bridge of the Starship Enterprise. Conveniently, they transform into recliners, beds, and traction racks. I found it quite comfortable to sleep on once I took a horse tranquillizer.

Everything in London is so steeped in history. For example, our hotel, the Dorchester, is where Elizabeth Taylor and Peter O'Toole had a sordid affair while she was still with Richard Burton in a separate room.

Do English subjects ever go to the dentist? I swear, most of these people could eat an apple through a tennis racket.

The BBC news department is on strike. But no one knows because no one's there to do the news.

Besides, everyone's watching *Celebrity Love Island* and *The Farm* instead. These reality shows feature marginal British celebrities – and by marginal I mean that Lulu is too big – embarrassing themselves in bikinis on Fiji or milking cows on a farm. In the latter show I thought the cast was dressing a warthog before I discovered it was fellow cast member, former American-porn star-now-pathetic-figure, Ron Jeremy. Gone are the days of Shakespeare and Dickens.

The real breakout hit at the moment is *Hell's Kitchen*, a reality show featuring a crazed chef named Gordon Ramsay. During the course of an episode he'll say "fuck" so often you'll think you're watching *Deadwood*. The public and the censors have no problem with this. But he caused a huge flack recently when one of his rants included the word "Jesus."

On the first night we ventured to the Comedy Store to see Omid do his stand-up act. Our cab driver began reciting JFK's inaugural address then followed with the script from "The Sting." It turns out he'd been in a movie himself, actually several of them. He was one of the kids in the Michael Apted documentary series that began with "*7 Up.*" He also was too big a celebrity to qualify for *Celebrity Love Island.*

Omid's stand-up was hilarious. He is indeed Iran's funniest comedian.

Went to dinner in Chinatown. I asked for tap water and the waitress shot me a murderous look. They were probably cooking dog in the back but my not ordering Perrier was a real affront.

Next day, David and I headed for the Underground to do a little sightseeing. We were side by side on the down escalator, unknowingly blocking the path. A gentleman tapped me on the shoulder and said, "Excuse me, I don't mean to be *pedantic*, but can I pass?" Can you imagine the same scene in a New York subway? "Hey, shithead, move your fuckin' ass!" New Yorkers hate it when you're *pedantic*.

Went to Baker Street to see the Sherlock Holmes museum. A number of American tourists were upset because they couldn't get into the house to see where he *actually* lived.

Next to the museum were an Elvis store and a Beatles store. Both were disappointing. No black velvet paintings in either. What's the point?

There's also a *Cheers* restaurant in London. You can sit at the bar with Norm, Cliff, and Field Marshall Montgomery.

Back on the "tube" to see Big Ben and Parliament Square. We asked a policeman where Westminster Abbey was and he didn't know. It was *across the street*. We stopped in to see some of our favorite tombs. I meant to check if there were any open slots. It might be kind of fun to be the only *AfterMASH* writer in Poets Corner.

There's actually a gift shop in Westminster Abbey. I was sort of hoping it would be next to Woolworth's tomb.

There's not a single person in this entire country that has a tan. The only people with color are drinkers.

The Queen Mother passed away in March of 2002. Out of the many thousands of messages left on the Queen Mum's Board of

Remembrance:

"She was a marvelous woman, and a wonderful lover." –L.J. Worthington, Penrith.

"She was one of the old school, all the remaining royals are shit." –J. Clement, Granthom.

"I was absolutely devastated, at least we could have got the day off." –S.Wilson, Bristol.

"Her death should act as a warning to others who think it is cool to experiment with drugs." –E. Franks, Cheshire.

"Perhaps if we automated her old golf buggy it could still drive around The Mall on its own and bring pleasure to the tourists." –Y. Howell, Slough.

I can honestly say that I have met Prince Charles. True story. He came to visit the *MASH* set when I was working there. We writers stood in a receiving line and when it was my turn I couldn't resist. I asked him, "What advice would you give young people thinking of getting into your profession?" He laughed politely then I believe he said to his handlers "This isn't *Charlie's Angels*. What the hell are we doing here?"

You can get hot tea, high tea, a spot of tea but no iced tea.

Actual log line to a BBC2 sitcom: *The Robinsons* 5-26-05 9:30 PM - "The family are amazed at what Ed's new girlfriend does to his nipples."

Went to a pub to watch Liverpool defeat Milan in the big European soccer cup. The town went nuts. "Good show! Good show!" There were celebrations in the street and unlike America, no cars were overturned or storefronts set on fire. These people are amateurs!

It was a jolly good trip, and hopefully we're on our way to a hit TV series. I sure hope so because I would hate to come back to London in a year and see Omid on *Celebrity Love Island*.

Cheerio…

NEW YORK

June 2005

A WEDDING TOOK ME to New York. Temperatures in Manhattan were a balmy 100 degrees with 100% humidity. And we're still weeks away from summer. The riots should come early this year.

Stayed at the Shelburne Murray Hill on 37th Street & Lexington Avenue. Major stars may stay at the Plaza, but guest stars of *Law & Order* stay at the Shelburne. So imagine my surprise when the elevator opened and it wasn't Tovah Feldshuh who stepped out, but Diane Lane! I wanted to tell her I watch selected scenes of *Unfaithful* at least once a week when I'm alone, but she was out the door before I had the chance.

The wedding itself was lovely. Held at the Chelsea Pier overlooking the Hudson River. It was *Goodbye Columbus* with a view. Every conversation featured the following words: lawyer, Hamptons, tumor.

There have now been more major league baseball games played at Shea Stadium than Ebbets Field.

Favorite Shea Stadium true story: Overheard a couple of years ago. A seven-year-old boy was in the front row. Between innings one of the Mets booster girls was on the field tossing free t-shirts into the crowd. The boy waved and yelled, "It's my birthday!" The coed didn't hear him. He yelled it again. "It's my birthday!" Still no shirt tossed in his direction. Finally, not to be denied, he screamed: "It's my birthday, *you cunt*!" Seven-years-old. Only in New York.

The "c-word" has now been uttered more times at Shea Stadium than Ebbets Field.

Our room was on the third floor. Annie suggested we just take the stairs. Yeah, right. Like I'm ever going to bump into Diane Lane in the *stairwell*.

Good news! The first 7-11 is coming to Manhattan. Over-under on the number of days until the night manager is robbed and tied up in the back: one.

Had lunch with my friend Chip Zien, who is now in *Chitty Chitty*

Bang Bang on Broadway. Apparently, the car in the show actually flies into the audience. How many people are going to be killed in high school productions of this musical?

There is now a Senor Wences Street in Midtown. Instead of a traffic light, a head in a box says *"sorr-riiiight"* when it's time to go.

On Sunday, I came across a BBQ festival. Picture this: four square blocks, a hundred booths (each grilling animal fat), a hundred degrees, steam rising from the subway grates, everyone smoking, surrounded by skyscrapers (so no ventilation), and PACKED with people. It's how I picture Hell or Arkansas.

On the way to JFK I visited my friend Matthew Weiner who is now writing and producing *The Sopranos*. He invited me to watch the filming. In the brief time I was there they shot three scenes and four actors.

Saw Diane Lane one more time in the lobby. I said something about even loving her in *Judge Dredd*, and she ran. Sigh. Only in New York.

SAN FRANCISCO

August 2005

FLEW INTO SAN JOSE on Thursday night to spend the weekend with Matt, who now has a great job at Apple Computer. (No, he can't get you iPods for half off.) Their campus is in Cupertino, the heart of Silicon Valley. Make a left at "Yahoo," a right at "Google," and it's a half-mile past the sprawling "Ask Jeeves" complex.

San Jose is known now as "Man Jose." If Surf City was "two girls for every guy," Man Jose is "a hundred guys for every girl" and "two girls who look like guys for every girl who looks like a girl."

Matt now lives in the Casa de Cockroach apartment complex in Sunnyvale. It's like the Oakwood Gardens except without the *good* drywall. And instead of a recently divorced man living in a one-bed-room apartment, here it's a three-generation Indian family of eight.

Silicon Valley is now filled with Asians and Indians. The many local steak joints do great serving one group but no business at all serving the other.

The Apple campus was most impressive. It's the Pentagon for nerds. Lunching at the company cafeteria, I couldn't help notice that everyone was either extremely young or 50-years-old, long hair in a ponytail, barefoot, and still living with their mothers. I counted maybe five women although it might've been eight.

For reasons I don't understand, street names just change random-ly. You're driving down Fair Oaks and it becomes Remington then Matilda. I'm told this is a plot to confuse the Asians and Indians but so far it hasn't worked.

Friday we made our way up to San Francisco for the weekend. Stayed at the Grand Hyatt at Union Square. Glad we planned on checking in late. We missed the four-hour evacuation and area street-closing for fear of a terrorist attack. Seems it was just a false alarm. Merely a big transformer that blew causing a huge explosion. But that wasn't the worst of it. Our room was so small!

Hyatt has the smallest rooms for any upscale hotel chain. Matt and I could barely walk around. An Indian family of only seven could fit in here.

Opened the window to see...fog. Anyone who pays extra for a view in this town is an idiot. I don't know why hotels even bother to wash these   windows.

Middle of August and it was 60 degrees. Mark Twain said it best: "The coldest winter I ever spent was the one summer in San Francisco."

I'd make a Rice-a-Roni joke but I bet half of you wouldn't have a clue what I'm talking about.

Public transportation in the Bay Area is fabulous. BART and Cal-Trains with their "baby bullets" make getting around a breeze. If only they had bullet Cable Cars. Those continue to go a mile a day. And you're wedged in like sardines. Each cable car is suited for maybe twenty people...or one entire Indian village.

Lunch at Scomas on Fisherman's Wharf is a must. Spectacular seafood and best view of the bait warehouse in the city. Be sure to stop by the bar and see their tribute to the most famous Italian crooner in history, Al Martino.

Fisherman's Wharf is filled with colorful street performers: mimes and jugglers, etc. Most unique was the "Shrub Guy." He hides behind a shrub in camouflage and when unsuspecting tourists stroll by he leaps out scaring the shit out of them. Meanwhile, other people observe nearby, laugh, and give him money. On a grander scale this is how Liza Minnelli now makes her living.

One shop at the wharf bakes loaves of sourdough bread in the shape of crabs. This artistic skill is right up there with rock candy blowing, chalk sidewalk portraits, chopped liver sculpting, and Presidential Advisor.

The Tonga Room is back! Nestled in the basement of the venerable old Fairmont Hotel, the Tonga Room was a SF tradition in the '50s and '60s. Last time I was in town it was closed for renovation – always a bad sign. But it's back and tiki-tacky as ever. Not just a Polynesian theme but with thunderstorms, indoor rain showers, a lake, and a group singing "He Works Hard for the Money" in Hawaiian. I placed my drink order by asking for anything in a skull. I would have said bring me anything flaming but that has a different meaning in San Francisco. We settled for Scorpion Bowls. An hour later we thought the rain was real. At one point Matt said, "If everyone forms a conga line then this will officially become my bar mitzvah reception."

The Cow Palace was aptly named this weekend. That's where they held open auditions for *American Idol*.

Stopped by Perry's for a drink on Union Street. Perry's is a SF throwback watering hole – Al Martino music plays, patrons bitch about the Giants, and you can almost see the ghost of Herb Caen falling off his barstool.

The Museum of Erotica is gone. So Matt and I didn't visit any museums.

Sunday we topped off our weekend by taking in an Oakland A's game. They were hosting the Kansas City Royals, a team so bad they just lost 19 straight – almost a record. A scalper in the parking lot was waving tickets, yelling "Sold Out!" There were enough empty seats to accommodate the entire population of India.

The best part of the trip was just being able to spend time with Matt. And for further reference, Rice-A-Roni is rice and pasta and dried seasoning mix in a box, created by the DeDomenico family in the Mission District. Their jingle was "Rice-A-Roni, the San Francisco Treat." Come on. It's the Rolls Royce of boxed food.

UTAH

August 2005

HERE'S A TRAVELOGUE YOU thought you'd never see – me in Utah. Along with my writing partner David, and *Frasier* co-creator, Peter Casey, I am writing a holiday movie. Peter has a condo in Park City, Utah and suggested we sequester ourselves there and really get some work done. So for four days I was in the land of the Osmonds and Gary Gilmore.

A stewardess was once fired for saying over the PA to passengers, "Welcome to Salt Lake City. Please turn your clocks back one hundred years." Landed in Salt Lake, did just that, then headed up the mountains to Park City, one of America's premiere posh ski towns.

The panoramas were positively breathtaking. I can just see a Park City man coming home from a hard day, stepping out onto his balcony, gazing at the magnificent vista and saying to his wives "Hey, Trixie, Jane, Gloria, Marge – you gotta get out here and see this!"

There's no snow yet so there are no tourists. Peter's condo is part of a gorgeous lodge. You walk down the deserted hallways, past the cavernous vacant dining room, through the expansive empty lobby and realize…

You're living *The Shining*.

All that's missing is the maze. But the quiet was most welcome and allowed us to get a lot of work done on the script. Thought you'd enjoy a preview. Here's one of many scenes we wrote:

All work and no play make Jack a dull boy.

All work and no play make Jack a dull boy.

All work and no play make Jack a dull boy.

All work and no play make Jack a dull boy.

All work and no play make Jack a dull boy.

All work and no play make Jack a dull boy.

I think we have another holiday classic on our hands.

Took a tour of nearby Deer Valley. Peter pointed out the chair lift pole that an expert skier crashed into, splitting open his skull. He also showed us the spot on the road where trucks spin off if there's a little ice on the ground. Later I learned that skiers on certain runs must carry beacons so if they're buried in an avalanche they can be found.

During the winter, reservations at most restaurants and emergency rooms are recommended.

Charles Gibson of *Good Morning America* owns a huge house on one of the hills. Circular and all in glass and chrome, it looks like the Cat in the Hat's hat. Jeffrey Katzenberg also owns an impressive chalet. I guess when he's not in Hawaii taking my lounge chair, he's up here.

Elayne Boosler says this about Utah: "My favorite store here is maternity gowns for Mother of the Bride."

REDRUM. I don't know why I just wrote that.

Deer Valley hosted the slalom portion of the 2002 Winter Olympics... although the event was held up for three hours because Jeffrey Katzenberg reserved that ski run.

David and I walked down Main Street in Park City (picture Knotts Berry Farm for rich people) and got a number of stares. I'm sure we were the first two Jews of the season. Kinda like the first robin of spring. Soon more Jews would follow and it would be ski season.

REDRUM.

Park City is the home of the Sundance Film Festival every January. For two weeks any rustic or quaint charm is completely obliterated as Hollywood agents, deal makers, opportunists, sharks, skanks, managers, hucksters, shysters, carnies, boot lickers, snake oil salesmen, and Katzenberg invade the area as if it were their own personal Bay of Pigs. But if you're a skier that's the time to come because no one is on the slopes. Which begs the question: Why not hold the film festival in summer when it's warm and there's no skiing anyway?

REDRUM. REDFORD.

During Sundance every theatre screens cutting edge independent films. The other 50 weeks they show *Dodgeball*.

There are almost as many SUV's here as in the parking lot of the Encino Gelson's.

Events I unfortunately had to skip: the "Howl-a-Ween Dog Parade" down Main Street featuring a whole pack of costumed canines. And the "Cowboy Poetry Gathering and Buckaroo Fair." I'm upset about missing that one because who writes better poetry than Gabby Hayes and Chill Wills? Plus they're going to have a colt start-

ing clinic (Is that some bizarre planned parenthood event?).
I can't afford a place here but my agent has one. Hmmmmm?
It stays dark every morning till eight make Jack a dull boy.
The ski lifts carry nobody make Jack a dull boy.
Most restaurants are closed and no play make Jack a dull boy.
All work and no play make Jack a dull boy.
All work and no play make Jack a dull boy.
All work and no play make Jack a dull boy.
All work and no play make Jack a dull boy.
All work and no play make Jack a dull boy.
All work and no play make Jack a dull boy.

SAN FRANCISCO

August 2005

THIS IS ACTUALLY A compilation of two recent trips up to the bay area to visit Matt.

As part of Debby's social work doctoral program at the Lilith Sternin Institute she had to attend a convocation the first weekend of October in beautiful Emeryville, nestled cozily between the hills of Berkeley and the gang wars of Oakland. We decided to fly up to San Jose, pick up Matt, and continue on to the East Baghdad of the Bay.

Headed north but veered off towards Emeryville. That's like bypassing New York City to vacation in Yonkers.

Emeryville is merely a collection of airport hotels without the airport. Why anyone who doesn't have a 5:00 AM flight would stay there is beyond me.

While Debby spent the weekend listening to lectures on dementia, Matt and I went to Berkeley to see the effects of it. The '60s are alive on Telegraph Avenue. It's as if a retirement village put on a production of *Hair*. Tie-dyed shirts, head shops, hat shops. What better father-son bonding experience than shopping for bongs together?

I hate to tell these people but the *Janis Joplin look* did not even look good on Janis Joplin.

A panhandler went up to Matt claiming to be Jerry Garcia. (true story) But when Matt didn't give him enough change, he proved to be a member of the *Un*-Grateful Dead, or at least the Not-*Sufficiently*-Grateful Dead.

Bumper stickers seen: *"Clinton lied but nobody died." "Impeach Bush," "FUCK LBJ."*

The Krishna's have a copier service. Considering they chant the same thing over and over, it's the perfect enterprise.

But Berkeley does have Amoeba Records, the Mecca of music stores. Now in three California locations, the Telegraph Avenue Amoeba was the first. And it's still the best place to replace your Dead Kennedys and Joanie Sommers albums. Only drawback: Everyone who works there is weird. And by that I mean Manson Family with a knowledge of show tunes and the entire "Biff Hitler and the Violent Mood Swings" catalogue. Dress code consists of Mohawks, tattoos, turquoise hair, tongue studs, and nose rings. What kind of sex life can they have when the only person who will ever touch their genitals is the one doing the piercing?

Telegraph Avenue was quite a contrast to University Avenue in Palo Alto, the Stanford equivalent, which Matt and I visited last weekend. Upscale, yuppified. The funkiest thing you can buy there is relaxed fit jeans at the Gap. Their sports bar has a sommelier.

We were there to see the big Stanford-UCLA football game. Bad enough the UCLA marching band tried to do a salute to Queen, but the team itself played like crap. And the stadium with its backless aluminum benches could not be more uncomfortable if it was designed for Al-Qaeda prisoners. So with Stanford humiliating UCLA 24-3 with less than seven minutes to go we did the smart thing and left. We beat the crowds, we beat the traffic…and we missed UCLA's stunning 30-27 miracle comeback win in overtime – one of the most dramatic finishes in the school's history. What a couple of SCHMUCKS!!!

For the rest of the weekend we did nothing but bang our heads into walls.

Meanwhile, Debby went into San Francisco. At Golden Gate Park she stumbled onto the "Wonder of Cannabis" festival. Everything you wanted to know about marijuana but had no more brain cells to remember. I'm sure a lot of former comedy writers had booths.

Stayed at the Galleria Park Hotel in the city. Charming or musty depending on whether you've been to the Cannabis festival. Our room was the inspiration for the Sam Spade pistol-whipping scene in *Maltese Falcon*.

There's not one radio station in town that will play Tony Bennett's "I Left My Heart in San Francisco." But six will play "Gangsta Sh**" by Lil' Eazy-E.

Hit the Original Pancake House in Cupertino. Try their famous German apple pancake. It's the size of a manhole cover and just one would give the entire Von Trapp Family diabetes. For something slightly less sweet you could order (and this is true) clam pancakes.

How could we leave that game early? What were we thinkin'????

Halloween weekend in San Francisco. You can imagine the costumes. It reminds me of the time I was announcing for the San Diego

Padres and we were in town to play the Giants. The team bus headed from the hotel to the ballpark but took a wrong turn and wound up in the Gay Pride Parade. The team couldn't understand why everyone was cheering. What a good sports town San Francisco must be!

Side note – Halloween: Jehovah's Witnesses do not believe in it. So the one night of the year when people would actually open their doors to them they stay home.

Must be sweeps. "News4 at 11" on Monday night begins a five part series on gang members now in the army. Will they return home and use their military tactics on YOU? And by that do they must mean will you catch them sleeping under *your* jeep?

Even though it was Halloween weekend I did not make it out to the Winchester Mystery House in San Jose. Built by some insane woman in 1884, this Victorian mansion has staircases leading to walls, hallways that go nowhere, fireplaces every which where, dead ends left and right, windows in interior rooms, etc. The Haunted Mansion meets the United Airlines Terminal at O'Hare. If they held the Cannabis festival there, no one would ever or could ever, leave.

Happy Halloween. And once again, how could we leave that game???

NEW YORK

November 2005

BACK FROM GOTHAM, WHERE I helped out on a musical called: *The 60's Project*, going into workshop production. It's a fun and poignant journey through the decade, complete with all the music and assassinations you remember. My main contribution was getting them to take "Who Put the Bomp?" out of the Tet Offensive section. But it's a terrific show despite an audience member calling it *important*.

Stayed again at the Shelburne Murray Hill. But no Diane Lane this time. They should tell you that when you make your reservation. Seven whole days I stayed in that dump!

The tree is back! The world's largest Christmas tree was delivered to Rockefeller Center this week. It was their second delivery attempt. The first time no one was there to sign for it, so they had to just leave a note.

Big Broadway show in town is the revival of *Odd Couple* with Matthew Broderick and, inexplicably, Nathan Lane as the slovenly *guy's guy* Oscar Madison. I know it's stunt casting, but Jesus, why not just go the whole way and cast Carol Channing?

Best panhandler: The guy at Broadway and 42nd holding a sign that reads: "YOU CAN YELL AT ME FOR A DOLLAR."

Close second: The Naked Cowboy. This skeesix has long blonde hair and wears nothing but a Speedo and a guitar. I would still believe him as Oscar Madison before Nathan Lane.

There is barbed wire around the Plaza Hotel. It is being converted to condos, but the Oak Room will remain. The city was able to get the upscale hookers, who were fixtures at the bar, classified as historical landmarks.

There's a Home Depot on Lexington Avenue in Midtown. How do people get anything home? They have to lug their new garage doors, or Jacuzzis, or lumber on the subway?

Went to Carnegie Hall for the first time to see singer Linda Eder. There are five balconies. The top one is above the Timber Line.

Scalpers could easily sell $35 top balcony seats for $2,000 by saying that they were the only Barbra Streisand tickets still available.

A hotel was bombed in Jordan, so currently there are extra security and SWAT teams at certain NY hotels. (Nothing at the Shelburne. They don't even provide valet service.) Now, for your $700 a night at the Parker-Meredian (actual charge this week), you are in the heart of the theatre and terrorist target district.

Debby flew in just in time for the "best sidewalk food vendor" announcement. A bratwurst hawker on Broadway who was presented his award and arrested for not having a permit.

Went to my favorite museum – the Margo Feiden Gallery, home of the glorious Al Hirschfeld collection. I was there so long I counted 4,362 Nina's.

Actual radio station press release: *Clear Channel Urban WWPR (Power 105) and Premiere syndicated morning duo Star & Buc Wild have replaced newsman "Crossover Negro" (Reese Hopkins) with "Chris the Queer" (aka Chris Hart).*

The MET LIFE building will always be the PAN AM building.

Debby was on the Seventh Avenue express train where a guy was going from car to car peddling his novel. I wonder if commuters would be interested in humorous travelogues???

Annie flew in from Chicago for the weekend. First stop was Long Island and a big gathering of Debby's relatives. We all met at an Italian restaurant on Queens Boulevard and had lunch. Just like a Sunday dinner scene in *The Sopranos* except Tony and the family never said *"No cheese, I just had meat," "what comes with that?," "are the capers fresh?," "I can make the same thing at home for fifty cents,"* and *"The last time I had cannelloni I went into labor."*

Stephen Sondheim came to our show on Sunday. And wound up sitting next to Annie. She'll be dining off that story for years. The performance went very well until one of the leads, in the middle of "Sugar Sugar" spotted Stephen and broke into "The Ballad of Sweeney Todd."

Joined the post-theatre crowd for drinks at the Algonquin Hotel. I ordered a *"Dorothy Parker's Suicide Device."*

Spending a week as part of the New York theatre scene was very heady indeed. Everyone was so friendly, so gracious. All of that will end of course when they find out I write for TV. But at least I met Stephen Sondheim. He and Annie are now exchanging recipes.

SAN DIEGO

February 2006

IN 1974, WHEN I was a disc jockey in San Diego, some idiot got the bright idea to call the city "America's last resort community."

Since I was looking for something to do as a last resort this weekend, San Diego was the perfect destination. I went to visit my good buddy and former radio colleague, Rich Brother Robbin. I never asked, but I'm guessing that's a fake air name.

Stayed at a quaint motel in Ocean Beach, right on the water. "Quaint" is another term for "Bates." For the perfect touch, on Saturday night it was a little foggy so a loud foghorn sounded from the nearby pier every thirty seconds all night long.

Ocean Beach is a terrific little throwback beach town. The main drag is Newport Ave. and is populated almost exclusively by mom and pop businesses. (The exception of course being Starbucks. I'm surprised there's not one in the Vatican). Black's head shop is exactly as it was in 1967 except they now take credit cards. As does the other head shop…two doors down.

There's a tanning salon, which seems a little odd since it's a block from the beach.

Other local establishments that the OB Chamber of Commerce recommends: Dr. Jefe's Body Piercing (see their website for patterns and diploma), Unbreakable Clothing, Karen's Consignment Gallery, Mallory's Consignment Gallery (that title was just too irresistible and catchy for one), Cow Records, and of course the Electric Chair beauty salon.

San Diego is a Navy town. Always has been. When WWII ended, troops from the Pacific came home via San Diego. Apparently the local residents were not thrilled. A red light district was growing, sailors were rowdy, not considered a good influence, and local leaders were complaining. The base admiral got an idea. For the next payday he insisted all personnel be paid exclusively in two-dollar bills. Within a couple of days the town was flooded with these two-dollar bills and local residents got the message. Sailors meant money. They've been embraced ever since.

Stopped down in Tijuana where, alas, no cockfights this weekend (probably in honor of Colonel Sanders' birthday). Purchased the really "in" designer drugs (the antidepressants that advertise in *Entertainment Weekly*; those people on Wellbutrin look like they're having sooo much fun!).

Swung by the Hotel Del Coronado, featured prominently in *Some Like It Hot*. It looks the same. Charming, classic, elegant, and ready to crumple like a house of cards if a gardener accidentally points a leaf blower at it.

La Jolla is the Republicans' Promised Land.

Skipped Sea World. No reason to ever go there without kids. They have a restaurant called *Dine with Shamu* where you can sit by the dolphin tank, watch Shamu do tricks and eat Mahi Mahi. Am I the only one who finds this disturbing?

There are more people in San Diego just sitting on the beach or their front porches, drinking a beer and staring out into space than in any other city in the world. No wonder there are two head shops and they're each grossing more than Sears.

San Diego's premiere strip club, the Body Shop is still in business, which is a relief because I still have my lifetime pass from 1974. Only problem is, the strippers from 1974 are still there.

And Belmont Park remains open – home of the Giant Dipper rollercoaster, erected in 1925 and restored…any time now. Appearing daily: Reverend Jim from *Taxi* – actually a hundred of them. They're the park employees.

For weather, sheer beauty, beaches, breathtaking panoramas, nice people, pretty people, and bag piping (another Ocean Beach available service), San Diego is "America's Finest City" - a far better slogan than "Last Resort Community."

FLORIDA

March 2006

THE SUNSHINE BOYS HIT the road. My writing partner, David, and I (only hours away from actually *becoming* the Sunshine Boys) headed for Naples in the Sunshine State to do research for our latest ersatz pilot.

We arrived in Ft. Lauderdale then headed across Alligator Alley. Didn't see any gators, but apparently at the first light of day they do wander out to the highway. The dumb ones try to cross. The smart ones stand along the side selling tickets to the world famous Sarasota Clown museum.

Were a studio paying for this trip we would have stayed in Naples. But since it was our own dime, Bonita Beach was our *Gateway to the Gulf* home. In the '20s there was this cult, the Koreshans, who believed that Bonita Beach was the center of the world. It was a celibate tribe so unfortunately it no longer exists. (Darwin works!) There's just a state park in their honor. And if I'm not mistaken, the Hampton Inn we were staying at is at the center of Bonita Beach, and room 229, just to our left, is the absolute DEAD center of the world.

No wonder the Holiday Inn across the street is proud. Their marquee proclaims "Number one guest rated shower heads."

Favorite store name (maybe ever): *"Master Bait & Tackle Shop"* on Bonita Beach Road. Yes, I purchased t-shirts.

You drive down Whippoorwill Lane and come to an intersection. On the left is a hospice; on the right is a nudist colony.

Everyone here is from somewhere else. A native is someone whose had to renew his Florida driver's license.

Florida is the home of many fun attractions. Disney World is okay but "Jungle Larry's Safari" in Naples is even better. It's a seedy zoo with drugged animals. During Hurricane Wilma last year some of the critters escaped. The spider monkeys got into the nearby Athletic club. The club wanted to get rid of them (their membership is restricted), but you can't kill monkeys within the city limits. I can almost imagine a rep from the club addressing a city council meeting. "In order to offset the damage of Hurricane Wilma and help our high school majorettes get to this year's Rose Parade, as a fundraiser we'd like to propose a cookout/monkey shoot."

Not to be outdone, there is also "Jungle Erv's Airboat World" - see the everglades mangrove jungle. With gift shop. I'm surprised funeral homes in South Florida don't have gift shops.

Other local attractions I missed: "Weeki Wachee," a live mermaid show and the "Dinner Train Theatre" where shows open out of *many* towns.

South of Naples is Everglades City. In the '80s it was the hub of a huge marijuana smuggling business. Eventually they were busted and 80% of the men in the town were indicted and sent off to prison. Well, now they're back and very bitter. It's a rough town. *Deadwood* with shrimp boats. Not the place for David and I to go to lunch and ask which theatre is showing *Brokeback Mountain.*

Big Collier County museum attraction: an old tank just sitting on the lawn. What makes it such a unique attraction is that it has a parking space.

There's a guy in Naples named Johnny who looks like he's right out of *The Sopranos.* Since he has an auto repair shop on the same street as a hospital, he calls himself "Doctor Johnny." His local commercials feature him in scrubs, standing over a sick engine, barking out orders to a buxom nurse. "Nusre, wrench! Stat!" Johnny's other job is city councilman.

Naples has a band shell but no concerts because of noise restrictions.

Under construction nearby is a whole new town, Ava Maria, funded by pizza czar, Tom Monaghan. Center of the town will be a Catholic University (are you picking up the theme here?) that will proudly feature the largest crucifix in America. *Jungle Jesus' Church Tour.*

They love their festivals in Southwest Florida. Among them is the wine festival, the harvest festival (who will be this year's Miss Vegetable?), and my favorite – the Swamp Buggy Festival featuring the "Mile 'o Mud" race, and the Swamp Buggy Queen. One lovely tradition is that once she's crowned she's then thrown in the mud.

Did not personally see the dreaded Skunk Ape, but a local resident claims this creature does exist and coincidentally resides on his property. He even has a blurred video. He's hoping to attract tourism. Jungle Larry is incensed.

There are 103 golf courses in Naples area. Only eight are public courses. If your ball goes into the rough, just leave it. The Skunk Ape might get ya.

EUROPEAN TRIP/CRUISE

May 2006

DEBBY AND I TOOK a Mediterranean cruise. Being the reluctant traveler I liked the idea that I could unpack once, just look out my window and the destinations would come to me.

The plan was to pick up the ship, Crystal Symphony (rumored to be the finest, confirmed by their brochure) in Lisbon, sail to Gibraltar, Barcelona, Sorrento, Taormina, Santorini, and ending in Athens. From there we'd spend a day in Athens (soaking up the ruins), two in London (getting soaked), and fly back home to L.A. Happy to report all went as planned. Except as I write this I don't know if it's 5:00 PM tomorrow or 9:00 AM yesterday.

Twenty hours traveling door-to-door from our house to the hotel in Lisbon. The most beautiful sight on the whole trip was our luggage coming down the carousel in the Lisbon airport.

Lisbon was fabulous. Someone told me the big attraction was butter. He's right. I wouldn't fly twenty hours for it, but as butter goes, yeah, pretty spreadable.

Lots of statues but none of Portuguese's most famous son – Davey Lopes. Despite winning a Golden Glove in 1978 and hitting 17 home runs *twice*!

Stayed at the Pestana Palace. It calls itself a hotel and national monument. Vasco da Gama had a weekly poker game in our room before setting out to discover the new world.

The "*Mediterranean* look" is very popular in Lisbon.

They also have a scaled down Golden Gate bridge and are constructing a "Disney's Adventures." Can Starbucks and an ESPN Zone be far behind?

No SUV's, which was very refreshing. Most of the cars looked like little shoes.

Saw an ad for the Champagne Club - "Lisbon's premiere gentleman club. Continuous table dance and striptease from 10 PM - 4 AM. Beautiful girls from all over the world. The ideal CORPORATE environment."

Boarded the Crystal Symphony for our luxury cruise the same day the last Titanic survivor died. It's a gorgeous ship. Much nicer than the Love Boat, and there were no sad washed-up sitcom stars wandering about (although at the start of the cruise, half the women did look like Florence Henderson, and by the end they looked like Roseanne).

They use 60 tons of foodstuffs for the ten-day cruise (59 for the Americans). The galley staff is 90. There is a guy who cleans fish for ten hours a day. The year I worked for Mary Tyler Moore, I envied that man.

Our stewardess, Vera, was very efficient. As a girl she was der Fuhrer's chambermaid.

The hardest working man in show business was our cruise director, Mr. Clean. Picture Dwight D. Eisenhower in an admiral's uniform, complete with Ike's tremendous flair for comedy. He comes from your typical entertainment background – Anti Sub detection unit in Vietnam and defensive linebacker for the San Diego Chargers. Not only did Mr. Clean host all of the evening entertainment, he was also the co-anchor of the ship's "Good Morning" show on channel 27 ("in the top of the news today, the scarf tying class has been moved to the Harmony Deck"), and the (dear God) "5:00 Funnies."

There are nine bars, the first one opens at 9:00 AM. And once a day there is a "Friends of Bill W." meeting (Alcoholics Anonymous). By the end of the cruise half the passengers should have attended.

They offer a Beginning Sushi class, whatever that is. Would have signed up but it conflicted with my "Folding Napkins" class.

First port was Gibraltar. Instead of paying a fortune for a ship-arranged tour we hired Arthur, a guy on the pier with a van. Other than the fact that Arthur should have been in a "Friends of Bill W." meeting himself, he gave us a great tour. The rock of Gibraltar consists of limestone formed hundreds of millions of years ago, or for the "Intelligent Design" people – last June.

From the top you can see Spain and Africa. Arthur thought he could also see Japan. "Friends of Bill W." Arthur.

There are 300 apes that reside on Gibraltar. None any cuter than the one that perched on my wife's head. They are amazingly smart creatures. One won ten Euros off of Arthur playing three card monty.

As for the city of Gibraltar – it's Catalina with a synagogue.

I always had this fear that when we left for the day sightseeing,

Vera was in our stateroom trying on my underwear.

Entertainment Tuesday night: A Judy Garland impersonator. I don't know, there's something really creepy about a Judy Garland impersonator who isn't a man.

Karaoke night – I sang a duet with noted FBI profiler, Clint Van Zandt. There was chemistry. I could feel it.

On formal night the Captain and his officers were introduced. I felt much more secure knowing my future was in the hands of the crew from *Das Boot*.

Favorite crew member name: Chief Electrical Engineer – Odd Magne Olsen.

Met some lovely people from Toronto, Croatia, and a couple that lives literally ten houses from us.

Port two was the amazing city of Barcelona (Starbucks on every other corner). Crystal offered a variety of guided tours. Those who signed up received a tag – BAR-A, BAR-B, etc. to differentiate their tours. As a result, all these people were walking around with tags that said BAR-F. Not really what you want to see on a cruise liner.

My wife continued her quest to visit the great museum gift shops of the world. One of these days we're actually going to go into a museum.

Unlike half the ship's guests we did not buy a bottle of Absinthe. That's a liqueur made from wildwood that is banned in the US because apparently it is, well, an opiate. So, now we had passengers thinking they're seeing giant lizards and gryffins. Or, in the case of crew members, an iceberg.

Stopped by a couple of the Gaudi designed homes (not to be confused with gaudy). He was a 19th century architect who was probably the first to work on Absinthe. All of his creations looked like a cross between Sleeping Beauty's castle, a Fun House, and Jimi Hendrix's final acid trip. Playful and spectacular; they are not to be missed.

Jesus Christ was taking pictures with tourists in front of the main Gothic cathedral. The fact that he's doing that these days, collecting street change, suggests that the bumper sticker is wrong – Jesus *didn't* save.

Strolled down the famous Las Ramblas shopping street, with its colorful stores, flower vendors, and cafés. Lame street performers. though. A guy who swallowed balloons. Name me a girl on Santa

Monica Boulevard who can't do that.

We had a medical debarkation while sailing by Corsica. Amazingly, there was no mention of it the next day on the "Good Morning Show." But Mr. Clean did say that Clint Van Zandt's lecture on "Famous Unsolved Cases of the FBI" was sure to be an hour of grisly photos and fun.

The problem with cruising was that, when you reach a destination, you have only a few hours to see everything, which of course is impossible. So, instead of a leisurely day of sightseeing, it was *The Amazing Race*.

Case in point: Sorrento, Italy, the Jewel of the Amalfi Coast. In one nine hour period we saw Sorrento, Positano, Amalfi, Ravello, had lunch, bought ceramics, visited the Hotel San Pietro, took pictures of the picture of Hillary Clinton, covered most of the countryside, stopped for fifteen breathtaking photo ops, shopped for Italian schmatahs, bought gelato, searched for more Absinthe, and toured Pompeii. *The Amazing Race* is easier.

We accomplished all this by joining two other couples and hiring a local taxi driver to be our guide and drive us for the day. Rafaele. We zipped around the Amalfi coast, taking treacherous hairpin turns and naming Grace Kelly movies. Blaring out of his speakers was the Three Tenors singing "My Way" and "Blue Moon."

Meanwhile, Rafaele pointed out all the landmarks of this history rich area. "Over dere is where dey do the movie, *Tuscan Sky* with Diane Lane." The castles and 500-year-old buildings probably were significant too, but we didn't hear about them. "Over dere is where dey do the movie, *Only You* with Robert Downey Jr. and Billy Zane."

Since there were not enough fossils on the ship, we had to see the ruins of Pompeii. 2,000 years ago this town was buried and hermetically sealed when Mount Vesuvius erupted and rained volcanic ash on it. At some point there may be another eruption, and 2,000 years from now archeologists will uncover all these people frozen with hand held audio tours pressed against their ears.

Didn't see the whorehouse paintings, which apparently are the highlight of the site. The perfect Ancient Roman "corporate" environment.

Truth in advertising: A chain of gas stations named AGIP. Considering the prices, "a gyp" is exactly what they are.

Stores in Italy close between 1:00 - 4:00 PM. Finally, a country that is husband-friendly!

For Mother's Day, I asked Vera to have a half-dozen roses delivered with a card. What a nice surprise when Debby entered the room and there were the flowers and the receipt. No note, but the receipt was very heartfelt.

Next port was Taormina in Sicily. Sicily, of course, is the home of the Mafia and pine nuts. They're obviously not very sensitive about the Godfather label. Saw a store called "Don Corleone Objects." T-shirts were sold featuring horse heads.

The picturesque city of Taormina is Pinocchio's village cut into a mountain. By this time my tolerance for "charming and shopping" was about eleven minutes. It used to be you would go through these little towns to find items you could not find elsewhere. Now, everything you could buy in Taormina you can get off eBay. Cheaper. So, after zipping through the main drag, snapping pictures we'll probably toss, we went back down to the beach which was lovely but disappointingly not topless. First, no whorehouse paintings and now this!

Yes, had pizza. No, it's not as good as Chicago's. But better than Tombstone's.

Back on the ship for "'50s night." All the waiters named Zoltan were dressed as car hops. The Vegas type show that night had a '50s/'60s theme. Eight of the whitest performers in the world belting out Little Richard hits. A gay tenor in a letterman's sweater saluting "the King." And if English is your THIRD language you shouldn't be singing Paul Anka solos. Picture Arnold Schwarzenegger: *"Oh vhy oh vhy can't vee tell dem, dis iz not a poopie lufff?!"* Highlight was the Connie Francis medley. 'Nuff said.

Everywhere you go on the ship someone is taking your picture. There's us getting on the boat, us getting off the boat, us hiding from Vera.

Other stewardesses folded guest towels into cute animals. Vera folded ours into swastikas.

Next destination: Santorini. The Greek islands have been the inspiration for many classic works of theatre and *Mamma Mia*.

Santorini is built on volcanic rock. According to legend (and Donovan), underneath is the lost continent of Atlantis. That's a stop on the Titanic's Mediterranean cruise.

The capitol city, Fira Town, rings the high cliff like a gleaming row of bottom teeth. To get up there you can either take a cable car for three Euros or ride a stinking donkey for eight. The Judy Garland impersonator took the donkey. *Oh, Judy suffered so!*

Don't shortchange Santorini by thinking it's just a party island. They manufacture great natural sponges.

More charm, more stores, more views, more churches, more steps, more ruins, more crowds. "God, this is spectacular. Let's go."

All kidding aside, I can't say enough about Crystal cruise lines. The service was phenomenal, and even though I'm sure the help resented us privileged passengers, they never showed it. If you're going to take a cruise, do it on Crystal…unless it's to Africa, where pirates attack ships. The only guns on board are the props for the *Les Mis* medley. Special thanks to our waiter Marinko and Vera for not killing us in our sleep.

Reluctantly, we debarked in Athens and immediately immersed ourselves in the local culture by checking into the Hilton. (Hey, we had Hilton miles. It was free.)

"Athens" must be Greek for air pollution. But the citizens don't notice because they're all smoking.

Couldn't have picked a better week to be in Athens. They were hosting the gala Eurovision competition. 38 countries were competing in an international singing contest. Imagine the worst of *American Idol, Up With People*, and *The Gong Show*. Abba won years ago and we're all still paying for it. Finland won this year. First prize was being able to occupy Norway.

Can't say much for the local hospitality. Two taxi drivers wouldn't pick us up, and we went into a café and were refused service because we weren't Greek. I hope one of the many Starbucks in Athens only serves Americans.

We could see the Acropolis from our hotel window. But decided to visit it anyway. Turns out it's more than just the site of the big Yanni concert, it's the Birth of Western Civilization.

Warning: It's a schlep. And most of the good statues have been moved to the British Museum. But it is a truly awesome sight. I mean, to see where Yanni actually performed for a TV audience of over a billion people – wow!

Warning #2: Between the number of tourists and the current

restoration project, it's better to buy postcards of the Parthenon than take your own pictures. There's no way to snap a photo and not have scaffolding and a crane in the shot, which detracts somewhat from the whole "antiquity" thing.

In the Parthenon's underground museum there is a sign that says: "No flash photography. No posing." To accentuate that point they show a drawing of a smiling girl with a big X across her face.

I was hoping to stumble upon a gyro stand that had a sign: "Established 430 BC. Refusing to serve Americans for 2200 years."

Flew to London Friday morning. Stayed at the Washington Mayfair. The lobby gives the impression it's a swanky hotel. Our room, however, was the flat Oliver Twist stepped up to when he left Fagin.

Be prepared for sticker shock. The US dollar is worth 40 pence. Best value: souvenirs at the London Bridge in Lake Havasu.

Tried to go to the Ritz Hotel for high tea, don'tcha know. Unfortunately there's a six to eight week waiting list. Pity. And we sooo wanted to pay $140 for two pots of tea and a finger cucumber sandwich.

For you ghoulish-attraction fans: the basement of Harrods has a memorial to Princess Di and Dodi. It's next to house wares. Don't miss it.

Oops! Last November the BBC forgot to renew their license allowing them to tape programs in front of live public audiences. Seems no one in the entire mammoth organization knew it had to be renewed. Last week they got busted. So now while they try to rectify that, all of their sitcoms and other audience shows are done before live audiences of BBC staff members. This includes a teen targeted music program. Today's hot breakout British bands are performing for a bunch of 70 year-old news writers.

Meanwhile, on Channel 4 there's a series called "99 Ways to Lose Your Virginity."

Finally a good restaurant in London! There's now a TGI Friday's in Leicester Square.

Went to the National Gallery…gift shop. According to the books on display there was an exhibition of American Painters in Paris 1860-1900. I wonder how it was.

Saw the new London revival of Sondheim's *Sunday In The Park*

With George. Good but no Crystal Symphony production. And no Mr. Clean coming on stage during curtain calls to remind us of the big art auction on the Lido Deck.

Caught up with Iranian funnyman, Omid Djalili. Also had dinner with Steven Moffat and Sue Vertue, the creators of my favorite sitcom since the last one I created – *Coupling*. Went to the exclusive Groucho Club. Seems odd that the man who said he'd never belong to any club that would have him as a member has a club.

And now we're back home with cherished memories, photos, new plates, butter, and a MasterCard bill the size of Portugal's national budget. But it was worth it. Except for maybe "'50s night." See you at Weight Watchers.

NEW YORK/CONNECTICUT

July 2006

I'M NOT IN MANHATTAN twelve hours when a brownstone blows up fifteen blocks from me. A Transylvania doctor/disgruntled husband, who took issue with losing the building to his wife in the divorce settlement, decided to detonate it. Hours before, he left his ex a message that read: "*You will go from gold digger to rubbish digger... I always told you: 'I will leave the house if I'm dead.'*" New York's finest is still looking for suspects.

Headline in the *New York Post*: "HONEY, I BLEW UP THE HOME!"

Snatches of cell phone conversations overheard while walking the streets on the Upper East Side:

Man: "*I dunno, then give him Novocain.*"

Little middle-aged lady: "*Well, it's not my concrete.*"

Woman: "*You don't fuck the landlord. EVERYONE knows that!*"

The theatre scene includes *Sleeping Beauty, Tarzan,* and *Lion King*. If Gershwin were alive today he'd be writing *The Mighty Ducks: The Musical*.

Stopped in at the Museum of Modern Art. This was new behavior: people taking cell phone snapshots of the paintings...and then moving on to another gallery...without stopping to even LOOK at the paintings. I guess the way to really appreciate Monet's mural length *Water Lilies* is on a four-inch screen.

I couldn't walk a block without encountering scaffolding. And yet I never saw a single worker.

On Wednesday, the weather was hot, muggy, stifling, and stagnant. People were going down into the subway for relief.

Saw *Spring Awakening* – a powerful, very erotic, and disturbing look at puberty and sexuality. It goes without saying that it was a musical comedy. It's set in 1890 Germany, so naturally everyone ends up either dead or miserable. Newcomer Lea Michele is someone to watch, and not just because she was naked.

Upper West Side: Hookers - $40.

Upper East Side: Tuna tartar appetizers - $40.

Best bargain and some of the best Italian food in NY: Ralph's at 56th and 9th. As my NY savvy friend, Howard said: "'50s atmosphere, '60s portions, '70s prices." *Molto bene and ring-a-ding-ding!*

More *New York Post*: In a recent edition, Christie Brinkley's affair with a teenager was the top headline. The Israeli War got second billing.

Player endorsements is one thing, but during a recent Mets telecast on Channel 11, David Wright of the *Amazins'*, in uniform, was pitch man for a miracle worker revival show, the kind where people throw down their crutches and walk. If this guy is so good how come Pedro Martinez is still on the Disabled List?

On to the Goodspeed Theatre, hoping what they say isn't true – that there's a broken heart for every street lamp in Chester, Connecticut.

Spent five weeks in East Haddam, Connecticut and nearby Chester, Connecticut where the musical I've co-written, *The 60's Project* is in production. My eternal gratitude to Michael Price and the super folks at the Goodspeed Theatre for their hospitality, support, and bug balm.

If you love Americana, "*the Nutmeg State*" is for you. Southeastern Connecticut was particularly beautiful and goofy.

Stayed at a lovely apartment. Very tastefully furnished. Naked drawings and statues throughout. Even the drinking glasses featured topless women. It's like I was in my own house.

A local pet store sells reptiles and "critters." And if you buy a cage they'll give you two free "long-haired dwarf mice." Excuse me but "critter" is another word for "road kill."

Roadside sign spotted: SCENIC ROUTE, NEXT 0.3 MILES.

A fork in the road – one sign points to Camp Beth El, the other to Christian camps.

"*Casual*" is another name for "*fried*" when it comes to funky fun seafood restaurants. Lenny & Joe's is the best.

Keep a can of OFF with you at all times.

If there's a ten-minute thunderstorm anywhere in Connecticut, power and cable goes off for the entire state. Usually for 24-30 hours. The state symbol should be a flashlight.

As green and lush and gorgeous as this place is in the summer, I bet the fall is even better. With all the salt in the Connecticut River, the red and gold colors of autumn must be extra striking and vivid.

If you go to Killingworth, take a drive down Roast Meat Hill Road. I'm not kidding. There's really a Roast Meat Hill Road.

The Merchant House on US 154 sells Vera Bradley apparel (e.g. purses) and fireworks. Ideal for m'lady terrorist.

My *60's Project* writing partner, Janet, got a manicure where the top coat was hoof veneer. Beware of any beauty parlor where their celebrity clientele includes Secretariat!

Boy, they love their Nathan Hale. One good quote ("I regret that I have but one life to give for my country"), and the guy is a god. Attractions include his house, his schoolhouse, his barbershop, and the Dairy Queen where he used to make Blizzards.

The Tylerville convenience store sells worms in the freezer section, between Ben & Jerry's ice cream and tater tots. There's something terribly wrong when worms are more expensive than long-haired dwarf mice.

Towns have colorful names like Moodus and Old Lyme (the actual home of Lyme Disease – visit their gift shop).

Good morning! The menu at a Middletown diner leads off with *"Breakfast Cocktails."* If you go out for pancakes, better have a designated driver.

Do not pass a market without stocking up on bug spray.

Big tourist attraction in East Haddam is the Gillette castle. I can just picture their knights, all using swords with the patented four blades for a smoother, closer kill.

All you see are people on motorcycles. What you never see are motorcycle helmets. They should rename one of the more treacherous streets Motorcycle Meat Hill Road.

If you bought a house here in 1792 you could sell it today for at least double what you paid for it!

There is better cell phone service in Antarctica than Southeastern Connecticut.

Had lunch at the Griswold Inn in Essex, which claims to be the oldest inn in America – serving since 1776. There must be a thousand old Inns on the East Coast making this same claim. There's an IHOP in New Hampshire that swears *they* were the first.

If you're hungry, haven't eaten in four days and only have one dollar, spend it on mosquito netting.

Larry, Darryl, & Darryl are alive and work at every gas station in the state.

A lot of these small towns look like movie sets. If you like bed & breakfasts, Laura Ashley-like dress shops, tchochkes, and cemeteries this is your dish.

Some big Indian casinos nearby. For you history buffs, Tony Orlando is appearing frequently.

There is a Goodspeed airport in East Haddam. One Cessna, a red shack that says 42B on the roof (no running through long terminals trying to make connections) and a burned out Quonset hut (the "Admirals Club"). It still takes two hours to get through security. The only airport employee is Grizzly Adams on a tractor demanding five-dollar landing fees.

Only passed through New Haven. Wanted to stop by that venerable jewel of the Ivy League, Yale, and tell the students to stop trying to be comedy writers. Go into law or politics for Christsakes! You're at Yale!

And never got to Hartford. Didn't want to fight all the tourists stampeding to the "Insurance Capital of the World."

But in five lovely weeks, I'm sure I saw all the major attractions of the Nutmeg State…except, now that I think about it, a nutmeg.

CHICAGO

September 2006

ANOTHER TRIP TO CHICAGO and Evanston to visit Annie.
Kama Sutra: The Musical and *Menopause: The Musical* are both
currently playing. Each is the story of Madonna.

There is a local chain called the Homemade Pizza Company. They
prepare frozen pizzas for you and you take them home. They have no
ovens. I can think of another name for the Homemade Pizza Company
- "*Any Market*"! I wonder if they offer delivery services: "Guaranteed
to arrive frozen or your money back."

Chicago is known for its great museums. Did not get to the
American Bar Association Museum of Law (didn't want to brave the
long lines), the National Asian-American Sports Hall of Fame, the
Leather Archives & Museum, or the International Museum of Surgical
Sciences (I wonder if they have a hands-on room for the kiddies?).

Don't book rooms off Expedia.com. Hotels allot them the worst
ones. At the Evanston Orrington, we were given the wheelchair access
room. The peephole, all the door handles, and clothing rods were
much lower than normal. It was like being in the Munchkinland
Marriott. The bathroom had no divider for the shower, so you'd turn
on the water and flood the bathroom floor. Thank God there were
handrails everywhere. Room amenities included a hair dryer, iron,
coffee maker, and can of WD-40. The featured movie on their pay-
per-view was (I kid you not) *The Ringer* about the Special Olympics.
I'm surprised their Hollywood Classics category didn't feature
Coming Home and *Born on the Fourth of July*.

One out of four Chicago homes have ceramic swans on their front
lawn. Why??? Maybe the first guy displayed one, his neighbor was
too nice to say how tacky and ridiculous it looked, so as not to hurt his
feelings he put one out, too. This was then repeated 2.6 million times.

We couldn't have timed the trip better. This was "Gun Buy Back"
weekend in Chicago.

Plans continue for "the Spire," that 150-story tower to be erected
on Chicago's lakefront. During winter windstorms that thing will

swing back and forth like a metronome. The developers say that's a good thing – your *views* change.

On Sunday I took the "El" to the Southside – where the stockyards meet the shore. Went to see the "other" Chicago baseball team play (y'know, the one that actually *won* a World Series in our lifetime). The White Sox were hosting the Los Angeles Angels of Some Other City in Fine Print. Considering the traffic on the Santa Ana Freeway, if you do live in Los Angeles and want to see your Angels, it's easier to go to Chicago.

"The Palehose" play in U.S. Cellular Field (formerly Comiskey Park). U.S. Cellular must've really paid through the nose to get them to change the name from "Park" to "Field" too. They announce on the P.A. that this is a residential area (mostly senior citizen assisted-living housing) and fans are asked to please leave quietly so as not to wake up the neighborhood. Then they shoot off deafening fireworks every time a White Sox player hits a home run. Even at 1:00 AM.

When kids on the street say, "Do you want to buy the *Tribune*?" they mean the whole corporation.

It drizzled for two days, which is only significant in that it crippled O'Hare airport. Since O'Hare operates normally at 97% capacity, all it takes are three raindrops to completely ensnarl air traffic. Another airport has been proposed to share the load but the site is forty miles south of the Loop, coincidentally near the residence of former Illinois Governor, George Ryan, who was just convicted on 22 counts of racketeering and fraud. So plans are on hold until 2013 when he gets out of Federal prison and wins re-election.

Even though the sprinkles stopped at 2:00 our 7:00 PM flight left at 10:20. There are so many delayed flights or cancellations that I bet on any given night more people sleep in the O'Hare terminal than every Holiday Inn in America.

The movie was *Rumor Has It* dubbed into Spanish. And snack boxes were $4.00 and included crackers. American Airlines says they know we have a choice in air travel, but they must think that only other choice is Uzbekistan Airways.

SAN FRANCISCO/NAPA VALLEY

October 2006

L.A. IS ALWAYS CRAZY nuts during the Columbus Day weekend so the lovely Mrs. L. and I decided to escape to Northern California.

Flew from Burbank Airport (now Bob Hope International Airport) Friday morning. Thank God the departure monitors aren't cute and say "On the road to San Jose," "On the road to Tucson," etc. It's disconcerting enough to hear "Thanks for the memories" when you take off. Departed from the Dottie Lamour terminal. Arrived in Oakland (Bobby Seale International Airport), which is now under construction for your inconvenience.

Struggled to find the rental car lot. No wonder we got lost. It's on Earhart Street. Who names a street after the most famous woman who disappeared and was never found?

The Hertz "Never Lost" system hated me for some reason. In the middle of the Oakland Bay Bridge it said, "Make a hard right turn. Now!!!"

This was Fleet Weekend with big air shows at the waterfront. Great fun. Gridlocked traffic and being strafed by the Blue Angels.

The Bluegrass Festival also took place in Golden Gate Park. Not that anyone heard any of the performers with an air show roaring overhead and the ground shaking.

Another great San Francisco landmark has bitten the dust. Tower Records at Columbus & Bay has gone belly up, a victim of the internet. This, two weeks after radio legend KFRC abandoned its heritage to play Ricky Martin records. If Janis Joplin didn't kill herself 35 years ago (or any day since), this would have done it.

After seven corporate sponsor name changes, Candlestick Park has returned to its original name – WorstStadiumInAmerica Park.

Big showdown there this weekend as the 49'ers played the Raiders. Week Five and between them – one win. Kinda like bragging rights between Spam and Head Cheese.

Had a lovely dinner Friday night in Berkeley only two blocks from the 119th shooting in the area this year – all part of the city celebration for the A's winning the AL division title.

Big sex trafficking scandal exposed. Who knew the Asian massage parlors (that seem to be on every block) were not on the up-and-up? Of course it doesn't help that most do have massage permits…issued to them by the San Francisco Department of Public Health. I wondered why those guys always seemed so relaxed.

Nearby, Modesto has a minor league baseball team. No joke, they're the Modesto Nuts. Seems the area is known for its dry fruits with one seed, testicles, and crazy people.

On Sunday drove to Napa Valley. Knew we were almost there when we saw the first outlet mall. If San Francisco is "Baghdad by the Bay" then Napa is "Tuscany by the Target."

EVERY place in the Napa Valley has a gift shop selling wine, candles, glasses, sesame mustard, and lavender soap. The Arco also offers brake fluid (But from '97, a really exceptional year).

There are 260 wineries in the Napa Valley. Mogan David is considered a soft drink factory.

Doesn't take long to get into that pretentious wine tasting spirit. Stayed at Villagio Inn, which was playfully articulate. Had dinner at Brix, which was saucy yet aggressive.

Didn't get to Coppolas's winery unfortunately. It's in Geyserville (or Geezerville). Was hoping Francis Ford would be there, greeting people and assuring them he could ship anywhere. And I could ask him what he was thinking letting Kathleen Turner try to pass for a teenager in *Peggy Sue Got Married*.

When you tour any winery you'll notice it smells just like that guy who is always out in front of your local 7-11.

There's a Jelly Belly Factory tour. If you go to a few wineries first you'll be saying, "Jesus, these grapes are chewy."

Skipped the hot air balloon flight. I just don't want my obit to read, "Died in a balloon."

All in all, a great time. We celebrated Columbus Day just like Columbus – by getting hopelessly lost at every turn. If Chris had had the "Hertz Never Lost" system they'd be celebrating his day in Rangoon.

NEW YORK

February 2007

WENT TO NEW YORK for a reading of my play, *Upfronts And Personal* on February 12th. I figured, what better way to celebrate Abraham Lincoln's birthday than in a theater?

On Fox 5's five-day forecast for Tuesday, it showed a low of 13 degrees and described it as "chilly." CHILLY??!! Are they kidding? I'm here to tell you, it was downright "*nippy*"!

But at least you can finally get a ticket to *The Producers*. Of course, it now stars Tony Danza. (I wish that was a joke, but it's not.)

It was "*Fashion Week*" in New York, although I obviously didn't get the memo (wearing a stocking cap that someone affectionately likened to a condom). The world's most successful bulimics converged on Manhattan to show off clothes only Nicole Richie could wear.

Taxi fares have gone up. And worse, some feature TV screens where you can watch *NY10: Taxi Entertainment*. Why look out the window and thrill to the sights of this vibrant city when you can watch NBC promos and horseracing bloopers?

New hope for troubled marriages – there's now a trapeze school on the Hudson River.

Stopped by "Ellen's Stardust Diner", a '50s themed Times Square malt shop where the waiters and waitresses all hope to be discovered by singing "Suddenly Seymour" on a constant loop. Please stop long enough to take my order!

Ellen's is the G-rated version of "Lucky Cheng's" where all the waiters are drag queens. "Suddenly Seymour" has a whole new spin.

A home-instruction schoolteacher billed the city for $5,864 for a 15 year-old-boy who died six months earlier. Her justification: "I teach dead people." Where she's going, she can tutor Al Capone.

Best panhandler in New York: A big black man with a sign that said, "MY PARENTS WERE KILLED BY NINJAS. NEED MONEY FOR KUNG FU LESSONS."

Ted Turner has a new restaurant – Ted's Montana Grill in

Midtown. He has a huge buffalo head mounted and you just *know* he'd like Jane Fonda's to go along with it.

The play reading went well. Now I can say *I've* had a play off-Broadway that closed in one night!

Didn't make it to everyone's favorite Indian fast food joint, "Curry in a Hurry" this trip. Maybe next time when Tony Danza is playing Frankie Valli in *Jersey Boys*.

HAWAII

April 2007

BACK FROM THE LAND where tattoos are not just a fad, reggae music fills the air, and you never see out-of-state plates – Hawaii.

Armed with sunscreen lotion almost confiscated at LAX, my wife Debby and I arrived at the Maui airport and sped off for the Kea Lani hotel in Wailea, passing a factory with two imposing black chimneys spouting smoke…or steam… or peyote. We figured this was a perfect time to go, before kids were done with school and TV executives were still stuck in affiliate meetings.

This was our first time at the Kea Lani (Hawaiian for "no shade"). A lovely luxury resort done in the Hawaiian tradition of Morocco. We chose not to stay in one of their private seaside villas that go for about $2,500 a night (but breakfast is included… just no seconds). A friend stayed in one and was told he was in luck. All new furniture because Charlie Sheen had just trashed the place.

There are three pool areas at the Kea Lani – an adult pool, a lagoon for families (read: screaming kids), and a drunk tank. This is a pool with a swim-up bar and let me tell you, the folks wading here were smashed out of their minds. Other than diving for fallen pineapple wedges, all these swimmers do is bob and weave to stay afloat…in four feet of water. There have been so many accidents however, that every day at 4:00 the red flag is put out.

True story: A guy took at a seat at the pool bar, water up to his waist, ordered a drink, and put a paper napkin on his lap. The message here: *Don't drink and swim.*

The first night we had a leisurely dinner at the hotel, under the stars, listening to the gentle sounds of the trade winds and a fire alarm siren. We sipped cocktails and remembered Pearl Harbor.

You know us! We biked down the Haleakala crater, rode horses in Makawao, kayaked through the coves of West Maui, hiked through a bamboo forest, surfed Kapalua, and snorkeled in a cove of sea turtles. That was the first morning. After that we did nothing.

For two days Maui was covered in "*Vog*" - emissions from a volcano on the big island (I forget its name. It had an "*l*," a "*k*" and sixteen "*a's*," five in a row). It blanketed all of Hawaii (except the very exclusive Four Seasons) with a slight haze/fog the locals call "*vog.*" Fortunately, from our terrace we could still see Molokai and the Ruth's Chris Steak House in the Wailea Shopping Mall.

All of Hawaii is still in mourning over the recent passing of Don Ho. There's even talk of renaming Honolulu International Airport, Don Ho International Airport. I'm all for it. Most cities name their airports after presidents or beloved politicians. This would be the first one named after a lounge singer.

Macadamia nuts are cheaper at Trader Joe's in Los Angeles than at Safeway in Maui.

In honor of the *Lost* season finale (filmed in Hawaii) the hotel did a fun thing. They abducted some of the women guests.

Every cabana boy on the entire island looks like Owen Wilson.

Condo ad spotted: "*Lovely unit. Two doors down from ocean view.*"

Real estate prices in Maui are through the roof. All the "haolies" want to move to Hawaii. Where do Hawaiians want to move to? Las Vegas. Who needs rainbows when there are nickel slots?

This sounds like a joke but it's true. At the Hawaii Theatre on June 17-20th they were presenting a production called *The Honeymooners: The Lost Episodes* starring local newscaster Joe Moore and Pat Sajak. "*To the mahina, Alice!*"

A synagogue in Oahu has the following website - "*Shaloha.com.*" I'm guessing they're reform. Stopping just short of having a pig with an apple in its mouth at the Purim Luau.

The Dali Lama recently stayed at the nearby Renaissance. (You'd think he could do better.) Wouldn't you love to be checking in and there he is going bonkers because they gave him a room by the ice machine? It would also be pretty cool to go to a Yoga class and there is the Dali Lama asking if he can share your mat.

Shaloha!

SEATTLE

July 2007

THE SEATTLE MARINERS GRACIOUSLY invited me to fill-in for a couple of nights on their radio broadcast. I arrived Wednesday during a record heat wave. 100 degrees. Who gets sunstroke in Seattle? It was like Tucson with ferries.

Seattle has only two things going against it – relentless rain in the winter and that God-awful Perry Como song.

Stayed at the Silver Cloud Inn. I know it sounds like the name of every character Iron Eyes Cody ever played but it was an excellent hotel. Rooms so comfortable you can sleep right through the freight trains going by all night. For whatever reason I always get the room by the elevator, or ice machine, or train.

Hey, they have Starbucks in Seattle, too! Who knew?

As I do every trip to the "Emerald City," I hit Elliott's Oyster House on Pier 56 for their amazing chilled cracked crab. Although with the heat, people were ordering them to put on their heads and down their pants.

The plan was for me to fill-in for beloved Mariner broadcaster, Dave Niehaus. For M's fans, that's like going to see a play and learning that Marlon Brando's part will be played by Regis Philbin.

I was to do play-by-play for three innings on radio. But on Thursday morning one of their other announcers came down with laryngitis and I wound up doing half the game alone on radio and the other half on TV. This particular telecast was also carried nationwide on Direct TV and worldwide on AFRTS. I hadn't done a television game in ten years so there was already an arctic breeze blowing up my sphincter. As expected, my first half inning featured a freak play that no one had ever seen including the longest tenured umpire in the history of baseball. It involved four runners, three missed tags, a missed base, three runs, a bad call, an appeal, all hell breaking loose, everyone scrambling for their rulebooks, and me calling it live. My FIRST half inning! I may be the only announcer to ever go to commercial break saying, "And the score after five – your guess is as good as mine."

Next night's game was much better. I did radio only and got a foul ball. It came into the booth, crushed our crowd mic and almost killed our engineer, but I got the ball so that's the important thing.

It is worth a trip to Seattle just to see Safeco Field. It's an architectural marvel – old time charm, modern amenities, spectacular views of the skyline and mountains, and a retractable roof. Players are begging to be traded *to* the Mariners instead of *from*. Traditionalists will enjoy the hot dogs, Crackerjacks, and Shiskaberrys (chocolate covered strawberries on a stick just like Ty Cobb used to eat). All that's missing are vendors going up the aisles yelling, "Lattes here! Get your caramel machiatos!"

Debby thinks Safeco Field should be renamed *"Coffee Grounds."*

She arrived for the weekend and the temperature went from 100 to 75. This is one of the many reasons why I travel with her.

"The bluest skies you've ever seen are in Seattle." Damn, I can't get that idiotic Perry Como song out of my head!

There's a local Ford dealer that features the *"No dicker, sticker."* Much better was the Minneapolis car dealer who once had the slogan, *"Bring your wife so we can dicker."*

If you ever have to use the bathroom in Seattle, stop by the Icon Grill. In the men's room there are three TV sets with videos of rushing waters – rivers, waterfalls, floods, dams bursting – accompanied by the "Ride of the Valkyries." Who needs Flomax? For you ladies there's an old high school health film warning of the dangers of *inappropriate* thoughts and *evil* deeds. Not that your date will be in the mood after going like a racehorse for twenty minutes.

Radio in Seattle has gone to crap since *Frasier* Crane left the airways.

Being a Mac guy I felt like I was behind enemy lines. But every store and gallery seemed to have an Apple computer. Bill Gates is not taking this lying down. A kid in Western Washington was hit by lightening listening to his iPod. Let that be a warning to you, Seattle!

Was going to go coho salmon fishing but they wouldn't let me clean the fish in my hotel room.

Also, didn't get down to the Tacoma Dome to see *Walking with Dinosaurs* – a stage show featuring fifteen life size dinosaurs (45 feet high, 75 feet long) making its US debut after trampling through

Europe. Finally a cast that Robin Williams can't upstage!

But I did get to Utilikilts in Pioneer Square for some new summer kilts. Yes, they're expensive but I save a lot of money on underwear.

Also in Pioneer Square, there's the State Hotel with a neon sign that boasts: "*Rooms 75 cents*." But check with Expedia, you might get a deal.

The Space Needle has a rotating restaurant on top so tourists may hurl while viewing any of Seattle's stunning attractions.

The *bearded sea captain with Popeye hat* look is still in; as are tattooed Joni Mitchells.

Stopped by Pike's Place Market, where the fish fly and the tourists buy. Did not go to the *Adult Superstore* right across the street. I did that once when I was broadcasting fulltime for the Mariners. Was with a friend, just browsing, and as I held up an Ass Master, wondering just what the hell it did, it occurred to me – I'm on television every night. This is probably not a place I should be seen in.

What *does* an Ass Master do?

The 520 floating bridge was closed all weekend for annual maintenance. So to get from Seattle to Bellevue you could only take the 90 bridge. A faster alternate route was to just go around the world.

Okay, yeah, well…the bluest skies I've ever seen *are* in Seattle.

LAS VEGAS

August 2007

MY WRITING PARTNER, DAVID and I are developing a project for Jon Lovitz & Rita Rudner, so we popped into Vegas to see Rita's show.

The big news is that Pamela Anderson is now magician Hans Klok's lovely assistant. I guess when Borat stuffed her in a sack her true talent was discovered.

Stayed at Harrah's – a hotel in search of a theme. I guess they thought all the good themes were taken, but they're wrong. Someday I shall open the Woodstock Hotel. I'll put up a big stage, get Richie Havens and Country Joe & the Fish impersonators and charge people $120 a night to lay down a blanket and sleep in a field. VIP accommodations nearest the outhouse.

The Harrah's slogan is *"Oh Yeah!"* Rejected slogans were *"Uh huh, Baby!,"* *"Don't Stop, Ooooh!,"* *"More like that!,"* and *"Okay, but you owe me!"*

Where else can you look out your window, see the Eiffel Tower, the Great Pyramid, dancing fountains, a tropical beach, King Arthur's castle, the Statue of Liberty, a pirate ship, and Berlin after the war (demolished hotel)?

There is a street bazaar of some sort outside Harrah's, recreating the great garage sales of Milwaukee.

Rita's show was hilarious. We hung with her backstage then were led to the best table. It was like being Ray Liotta in *Goodfellas* without having to marry Lorraine Bracco.

Most cities celebrate history with museums. Vegas pays tribute to our nation's past with the only remaining Playboy Club.

And there's now a Hooters Hotel. Call and ask to speak to John Smith. They'll ring up 450 rooms.

All you have to do is watch the people who waddle through any Vegas casino, cup of quarters in one claw and a churro in the other to see why *The Wire* didn't get any Emmy nominations.

Stopped by the Imperial Palace, which quite frankly is neither. If

T-Bag from *Prison Break* wanted to gamble in style on the strip this is where he would go. But the Palace is no longer owned by that guy who proudly had Hitler's town car on display. And they're the only hotel with *Dealertainers* – celebrity impersonators (Elvis, Sinatra, Barbra Streisand, etc.) who also deal blackjack. Where's Stevie Wonder's table?

There is now always a World Series of Poker going on.

Good news for old Jews! A Fontainebleau Hotel is coming soon. In no time you'll be banging your spoons to Mitzi McCall, Rich Little, Abbe Lane, and Elliott Yamin.

The Celine Dion "Cheese-a-palooza" continues to assault and stupefy audiences at Caesar's. Imagine the Orange Bowl Halftime show, the Olympics Opening Ceremony, the West Hollywood Gay Pride Parade, and Mt. Vesuvius erupting all rolled into one. And that's just as they're seating you.

Carrot Top is a Vegas headliner. Somewhere in the great beyond Bugsy Siegel is saying, "*If this is what I ultimately created I deserved to be shot.*"

It is a town unique to the world. Come for the glitz, stay for Rita Rudner, and hang around till Saturday when Gerry & the Pacemakers headline at Cannery Row. Las Vegas truly is Chuck E. Cheese for adults.

DALLAS

August 2007

BACK FROM TEXAS, DEEP in the heart of. Spent the weekend in Big D, speaking to the Dallas Screenwriters Association, filling in for the Mariners (in town to play the Rangers), and risking gout with every meal. On every corner there's either a steakhouse or a church. One place called "Holy Cow" could be either or both.

The current Dallas motto is *"Live Large, Think Big"* which is much better than the more accurate: *"Not Just Hot, But Humid."*

Believe it or not, Dallas has more restaurants per capita than New York City (although NYC has a huge lead in salad bars) and more shopping centers per capita than any city in the U.S. *"Eat Large, Spend Big."*

Dallas is a surprisingly cosmopolitan city. Gorgeous downtown skyline, with its tall towers outlined in shimmering green and white lights. There are museums, a night life, and be careful going to that shit-kicker bar, it just might be gay.

Not to further tarnish Dallas' proud redneck reputation but until recently their mayor was a woman…and Jewish, Laura Miller. And in 2004, Lupe Valdez was elected sheriff of Dallas County. She's the first Hispanic, first woman, and first lesbian to ever fill that role. Hey, she might've had better luck getting into Miss Kitty's bloomers than Marshall Dillon ever did.

Stayed at the Arlington Hilton and had a lovely view of people throwing up from 700 feet on the *Six Flags Over Texas* thrill rides. Nearby is *Hurricane Harbor*, a waterslide amusement park. I'm sure it's very refreshing if you pretend that hundreds of people don't pee in it everyday.

Football is king in Dallas. High school games routinely draw from 20 - 50,000 people. And still, no one watches *Friday Night Lights*.

Meanwhile, the entire world stops for the Dallas Cowboys. Last week when the Rangers broke an all-time major league record by scoring 30 runs in one game, they still shared the front page of the sports section with the Cowboys training camp report on wind sprint drills.

In Arlington, they're building a new stadium for the Cowboys, affectionately known as *Jerry's World* (for Jerry Jones, the team's owner). It's costing in the neighborhood of one billion dollars, will have a retractable roof, and the two largest glass panels in the world. Which makes sense financially because the stadium *will* be in use eight times a year.

Had to once again see the Texas School Book Depository (now an excellent museum) where Oswald shot Kennedy. Forget that it's across the street from a Morton's Steakhouse, it's still pretty chilling. On the street itself are X's where the shots landed. I don't think they needed the guys standing around selling grisly pictures, however. America remembers and profits.

Saw the grassy knoll and the white picket fence that hid the alleged "second shooter." But it's not the original picket fence. It's a replica. The real one I understand (true story) was sold on Ebay.

Meanwhile, I'm still waiting for the Conspiracy Museum to reopen. Their previous landlord booted them out – a plot no doubt engineered by the CIA, Rupert Murdoch, Korean airlines, and Posh Spice. I hope my phones aren't tapped because I wrote this.

If you go to *Black Eyed Peas'* and order your first chicken fried steak (like I did fifteen years ago when I was fulltime with the Mariners), don't ask them to cook it "medium rare." I did and it was an E.F. Hutton moment as forty Rooster Cogburns stared at me in utter disbelief.

When you think of Dallas – what comes to mind besides JFK, football, cured meats, heat prostration, people carrying weapons, the Trammell & Margaret Crow Collection of Asian Art, rodeos, rodeo clowns like our president, country clubs, "Country" Charlie Pride, evil oil companies, the Renaissance Hotel that looks like a Bic lighter, J.R. Ewing, Dr. Pepper, Texas-Instruments, SMU, Verne Lundquist, the first Neiman Marcus, the Savings & Loan crisis, Tex-Mex, cheerleaders, and "Debbie Does?" Why radio station jingles of course! Dallas is the home of JAM Creative Productions the largest radio jingle mill in the country. Big D is filled with gifted singers who would all have huge careers if they could only sing songs that were longer than eight seconds.

There's a chain of convenience stores called "Grab and Go." I guess their target customers are robbers.

And the police have recently instituted a "no pursuit" rule so it's "Grab and Go At Your Leisure."

Goff's Hamburgers no longer has an eight-foot statue of Vladimir Lenin out front. I don't know about you, but nothing says tasty burgers to me like the Russian Revolution.

If you want tacos there's Taco Bueno, Taco King, Taco Cabana, Taco Bell, Taco Diner, Taco Express, Taco Grande, Taco Pronto, and Taco Loco Wagon. If you want a good deli, good luck. It's easier to find a mountain in Dallas.

For Italian, there's the aptly named Campisi's Egyptian.

My dining trips took me to Pappadeaux, which was excellent (I find the more unpronounceable the title, the better the Cajun cuisine), Lawry's for a light lunch of prime rib, and Sonny Bryan's Smokehouse BBQ, clogging Dallas arteries since 1910. *"Live Large, Think Pig."*

Mark Cuban, billionaire owner of the Mavericks, supposedly answers his e-mail. Not true. I dropped him a note saying I'd be in town, and wondered if he could show me Bonnie Parker's grave. He never responded, the bastard.

How perfect! There's a highway named for George Bush… and it's a toll road.

Guns are not allowed in bars or libraries (without silencers).

Sunday night I filled in for the great Dave Neihaus and broadcast the Mariners-Rangers game back to Seattle. It was my first time in the Rangers' new stadium. Originally named "the Ballpark," they must've felt that was too generic because they've now renamed it the far more colorful, "Rangers Park." What they really should call it is "the Typhoon." My God! It was like the movie *Twister*. I fully expected to see a cow fly by the booth as I was describing the action.

I would've gained twenty pounds if I didn't stop off at *Six Flags Over Texas* for some thrill rides on my way out of town.

"Live Large…or Think Bulimic."

BIG SUR

October 2007

TWICE A YEAR MY wife has to go up to Berkeley for an academic conference, so we took the opportunity to have a romantic night in Big Sur, visit our son in Silicon Valley (where he's designing the new Apple iSomething), and have a leisurely weekend getting lost thanks to the Avis GPS system.

Rented my first Prius at the San Jose airport. For an extra $10 a day you can get one with Oregon plates so you'll *really* look like you're going green. It would've been nice if Avis had included an owner's manual. Questions I never solved: why did the little exclamation point warning light come on? What does it mean? And how do you get the car out of reverse?

Big Sur is absolutely breathtaking. And the drive to it on winding single-lane California Highway 1 offers spectacular views if you can just get by the traffic, gusty winds, septic tank trucks, construction, vertigo, panic attacks, drizzles, car sickness, and bikers.

You've seen Deer Crossing signs? There is a Pig Crossing sign on Highway 1.

Since the area is so stunningly gorgeous they take their New Age star gazing, crystals, plain-aired painting, scented candles, and Yanni very seriously. That'll change when Walmart moves in.

Stayed at the Ventana Inn & Spa, which is my idea of "*roughing it*." A plasma TV and wireless internet is a *must* for this hearty outdoorsman. Sure the fireplace wood was pre-chopped, treated, and in a convenient burlap bag, but I had to *light* it. Well…actually my wife lit it.

They have a clothing optional pool, which is wrong on so many levels. Let's just say this is where the Pig Crossing sign should be.

Did not sign up for the mushroom hunting expedition, which reminds me, lots of old hippies still make Big Sur their cave. They can all show you Bobby Darin's former trailer and where Jack Kerouac – all hopped-up on espresso – wrote his greatest novel (until it was explained to him that someone else had already written *Little Women*).

The drive back up to the Bay Area was equally treacherous/lovely. Swung by storied Pebble Beach golf course in Monterey. I could almost hear the ghost of Bing Crosby saying to his caddy, "Hey, hand me a five iron, willya? Think I'll beat Gary senseless with it."

From the mean streets of Carmel comes this from their police blotter: "*Parking complaint/violation of box delivery truck blocking in numerous cars in the Carmel Center parking lot. Driver found but had a disrespectful and cavalier response to complaining parties. His employer has been contacted/warned.*" You'd think former mayor Clint Eastwood would have cleaned up this shameful lawlessness!

The Carmel Middle School was holding its fifth annual "*Solar Tour & Sustainability Fair.*" It's as if Al Gore planned a Halloween Carnival.

Got out of there just before the moth spraying. Moths? Still??? What the hell did Mayor Clint DO for four years???

Drove past Santa Cruz. Lovely woodsy area. In California anytime you have a region with more than one hundred trees it is required by law that there be a Santa Claus Lane.

There is not one Coffee Bean in the entire South Bay. However, Matt says there is one in Shanghai.

Palo Alto was going nuts Saturday night after the Stanford football team, a 41-point underdog, upset mighty USC. Crazed rowdy students filled the bars on University Avenue yelling, "Imported lager and Irish Red ale for everyone!"

From the "*Summer of Love*," San Francisco has moved into the "*Fall of Maybe We Should Start Seeing Other People.*"

When in Berkeley, NEVER stay at the Doubletree Marina. There is a buoy in the bay that rings a bell every 30 seconds ALL NIGHT LONG. The homeless guys on Telegraph Avenue get a better night's sleep than anyone staying at the Doubletree Marina.

Unfortunately, I was one week too late for the Folsom Street Fair in San Francisco. The Folsom Street Fair is a celebration of leather culture and sexual fetishism (not to be confused with the Carmel Middle School "*Solar Tour & Sustainability Fair*"). There were the usual couples leading each other down the street with dog collars and leashes, public floggings, men in thong underwear playing Twister, women dressed in teeny silver dresses shaped like martini glasses and bra cups decorated like green olives, and for the shoppers, stalls selling such must-have items as baseball caps reading "*Master*" or "*Slave*," silk ropes for being tied up, and a book entitled *Dungeon Emergencies and Supplies*. "*The Solar Fair*" offered recycling tips.

It was a hectic but fun four days. And to answer your next question: 40.3 mpg. But I understand you get even better mileage if you're in drive.

LAS VEGAS

December 2007

DEB AND I JUST GOT back from a brief weekend in Las Vegas, or, as I like to call it, "Three Card Monty for the Red States." Many big attractions there this weekend. The annual rodeo, the Anti-Aging conference, the Jose Luis Castillo/Joel Casamayer title bout. But we were there to see Linda Eder. Ms. Eder is a spectacular singer – Barbra Streisand but at affordable prices. And you never have to suffer through "Evergreen." We've become friends with her manager, Dave, who graciously invited us to join him for her concert. Since we likely would have gone for the rodeo anyway, we gladly accepted.

Stayed at the Mandalay Bay. Dave is also a VP of something for the House of Blues (who knows more about the blues than the Jews?) and arranged for us to get a room on the "House of Blues" floor. It had the two things Debby and I require in a hotel room – a fabulous view and voodoo decor.

I'm not joking about the annual Anti-Aging conference. But am I the only person who finds it odd to hold an Anti-Aging conference in the one place where people stay up all hours drinking, gorging, smoking, and enduring the enormous stress of losing their money? I guess it's held there out of respect for Joan Rivers. My feeling is if the president of the Anti-Aging organization isn't 117 then it's a sham.

Had dinner Friday night at Rumjungle in the hotel. Girls dance in cages above your head. To me that is tacky. To Vegas it's positively elegant.

Interesting crowd at the hotel because of all the special events. A lot of shitkickers (I assume for either the rodeo or *Mamma Mia*) and the prizefight attracted several hundred Ruben Studdards decked out in bling and Oakland Raider sweatsuits.

Next day we hit the beach. Yes, Mandalay Bay has its own beach. Unfortunately, the ocean was turned off. No waves. But Debby and I took a long walk along the grid that serves as the shore and gazed out at the horizon to see the Lance Burton Magician billboard on Las Vegas Avenue.

From there we hotel hopped. Had to stop in at the Excalibur – a casino in Sleeping Beauty's castle. This is home to the black socks, shorts, and wife-beater shirt crowd. You know you're in trouble when they have a special parking lot just for motor homes. Handing a pair of dice to one of these idiots is like handing a gun to a monkey.

Then on to the Bellagio, where Debby and I checked out the Monet exhibit at their fine arts gallery. (How can you go to Vegas and not stop in a museum?) I imagine when most of the tourists saw the ad for the exhibit they said, "Hey, they spelled money wrong!"

The highlight of the trip was the Linda Eder concert. It's the third time I've seen her. I realize one more time and I'm officially gay. But I don't care. The only problem was that her concert hall was impossible to find. It's somewhere on the University of Nevada at Las Vegas campus – *the Jerry Tarkanian Music Hall*, or something like that – and even cab drivers have no idea where this is. Dave and I set out for the sound check. The venue is five minutes from our hotel but we wound up somewhere near the Mustang Ranch.

Headed home early this morning. McCarran airport is the worst in the country re security checks. You actually *do* have to allow two hours. It's bad enough you have to remove your shoes, but the spurs must come off too, and that takes some time.

And now we're home, shopping for voodoo wallpaper.

FLORIDA

March 2008

ONE OF THE JOYS of my new assignment as host of Dodger Talk on KABC is getting to go to spring training in Florida, and one of my joys as a dad is being able to bring my son along with me. For five days Matt and I drove around the state, went to ballgames, watched ballplayers in their natural habitat, and bonded as only a father and son can. At Hooters.

First stop was Ft. Myers. It's in the county with the highest foreclosure rate in the nation. You could *feel* the civic pride.

Ft. Myers is the spring home of the Minnesota Twins and Boston Red Sox. I saw a thousand people wearing Red Sox hats and jerseys. The only time I saw the Twins logo was on a really scary rally monkey in a CVS pharmacy.

Stayed at the LaQuinta Inn. There's a sign in the elevator: "In case of fire – *run.*"

People think of Ft. Myers as a beach community, or a golf community. No, it's the home of furniture stores. Hundreds and hundreds of furniture stores. No wonder there are so many foreclosures. In every condo there must be seven divans, eleven coffee tables, and three dining room sets. Who has anything left for mortgage payments?

Ft. Myers is also where Thomas Edison invented the phonograph, so it's the birthplace of music piracy.

Hit the Dodgers-Red Sox game on Thursday at City of Palms Park, not too far from the estate of noted anti-Semite, Henry Ford. It was a typical well-played spring game with the Dodgers scoring seven runs in the ninth inning off of two pitchers who will spend the summer as mop up men in a beer league.

On Friday we took in the Red Sox game, and sat with ESPN baseball guru Peter Gammons, who told us some great stories like the kid who played winter ball in Venezuela and mailed an entire shipment of cocaine to the team's spring training facility. He's in the outfield one day during a game and seven federal agents call time and take him away in handcuffs.

The three-hour drive across the state through *Deliverance Country* went without incident.

Caught up with the Dodgers again Saturday to do my first of two daily radio shows. "Dem bums" were at Jupiter to play the Cardinals. There was nowhere to sit. You'd think with all those goddamn furniture stores in this state they would have a few chairs.

In the seventh inning a vendor yelled out, "Last call for beer and soda!" Soda??? People can't drink soda after 3:00 PM?

Jupiter is where Burt Reynolds had his dinner theater from 1979 to 1997. And now there's a Burt Reynolds museum. All the memories, all the hair pieces, and a look back at the storied career of a man who slept with both Dinah Shore and Sally Field.

On to Vero Beach after the game. Thought I saw a motorist failing a breathalyzer test for having one Pepsi too many.

This is the Dodgers' final season at Vero Beach. For 60 years they've been coming to this converted World War II naval base, and it is finally sinking in why the Navy chose this location. It takes forever to get to it. No Axis Power army would bother. You can understand why even diehard fans from Los Angeles get as far as the Epcot Center and bag it.

But if you do arrive, it is baseball heaven. Fans can stand right by the batting cages and practice fields. It's your chance to call a guy "a piece of shit" and have him actually *hear* it!

Streets in the complex are named after Dodger Hall-of-famers. "*Jackie Robinson Avenue*," "*Duke Snider Drive*," "*Vin Scully Way*." Next year the Baltimore Orioles might take up residence there. Somehow it won't be the same walking down "*Boog Powell Road*," "*Moe Drabowsky Boulevard*,"or "*Gus Triandos Way.*"

Larry King was on hand for Sunday's game. He threw out the ceremonial first wife.

Some things I learned about Vero Beach:

All Christian chapel services at Dodgertown are held in the Sandy Koufax room...

Tommy Lasorda actually believes half the things he says...

Sex is known as "night fishing."...

Sandy Koufax used to throw his curve ball by holding the baseball between his second and third fingers. You try that. It can't be done...

Early bird dinner specials in Vero Beach begin at noon...

Did our three-hour radio show from the press box Sunday night. We were on the scene live to call the action if a fan, who had too much Tommy Lasorda wine, snuck onto the field and took a pee.

Drove to Orlando on Monday to reluctantly fly home. I found it amusing that just after you pass Disney World ("For children of all ages") there's a billboard for *Vasectomy.com*. Trust me, after twelve hours of wrangling over-stimulated children you don't need the billboard.

If you turned in an Avis car needing gas, they charged $7.20 a gallon. If you went to the gas station right near the rental car return locations it was $4.60 a gallon. But if you drove another two blocks (like we did), it was $3.19.

This was one trip I hated to see end. So many laughs and stone crabs. And as a lifelong Dodger fan it was very special for me to be able to introduce my son to the Dodger players. I just wish he wasn't wearing his Red Sox sweatshirt that day.

CHICAGO

June 2008

IN CHICAGO FOR ANNIE'S graduation from Northwestern. It's been a busy final week for her – a prom, rehearsals, changing her major one last time. And a hectic week for us. Usually when my wife and I travel we don't also include my son, father, brother-in-law, sister-in-law, and seven-year-old niece-in-law.

The eight of us arrived on four different flights at four different times. Each flight was late, rides were missed, and thus began five days of what I like to call *"the Chinese Ringtone Torture Test."* My wife's cell phone died so all calls went through me. I was Heidi Fleiss during Super Bowl weekend.

Our hotel in Evanston, normally at $115 a night charged $335 a night for graduation weekend. And you needed to make your reservations the day your child got her acceptance letter.

Evanston was packed for the festivities. The panhandler in front of CVS pharmacy snarled, "I can't wait 'til you people get out of here! No one from out of town gives me a dime!"

Restaurants loved it though. Even Ruby Tuesday's was taking reservations.

The good weather season in Chicago is June 21st so we timed it pretty well. When the sun is out and people aren't collapsing from the heat and humidity, a favorite activity is street fairs – coating every building with a smoky layer of grease. Wasn't able to get to any this go-round but the one I really wanted to see was the Caribbean Jerkfest. In LA we have the Hollywood Jerkfest, but it's normally just called "The Emmys."

Of course it did rain during the outdoor graduation ceremony. I think it was God's way of punishing Northwestern for no longer calling themselves "the Fighting Methodists" (They really once did).

They should go back to it. Maybe they'd get to a bowl better than the Alamo or Citrus. Instead of Willie the Wildcat, their mascot could be someone in a Tallulah Bankhead costume with ninja sticks.

Not to get too wrapped up in tradition but this was the 150th time

Northwestern graduate candidates filed in, all in cap and purple gowns, all on cell phones. A few with iPods. Only one or two with a Wii.

I honestly didn't think this day would ever come. I never really believed I'd see my daughter spend two hours in a football stadium.

We helped pack up Annie's apartment. She shared it with two other classmates so there was a lot of sorting. "Annie, which of these empty gin bottles is yours?" It's amazing how many pirate decorations you can accumulate in only four years. I'm not sure whether new students are moving in next year or they're just condemning the building.

Al Capone is still more popular in Chicago than Sammy Sosa.

Sunday was a delightful mix of sunshine and hail.

I've loved going to Chicago these last four years. There are a lot of things I'm going to miss, including: ribs, the people, Wrigley, Rush Street on warm nights, the Jack Brickhouse statue, Gino's, the view from Sears (the tower not the Auto Center on Cicero Ave.), Bob Hartley's apartment building, Ed Farmer, the National Asian-American Sports Hall of Fame, Frank Lloyd Wright, egg salad recalls, Le Peep's, whatever Marshall Fields is called these days, Gene & Georgetti's, Lyle Dean, Lakeshore Drive, the Pat & Ron show, Dixie Kitchen, Bill Kurtis, everyone talking like Joan Cusack, cab driver Robert who learned to speak English by watching *Major Dad*, Flat Top, the International Museum of Surgical Sciences, Roger Ebert in the *Sun-Times*, the panhandler in front of CVS, the Purple Line to the Red Line, John Records Landecker, and finally – just hangin' with my BFF, Oprah.

Go Fighting Meths!

HAWAII

February 2009

JUST BACK FROM A month in Hawaii. Yes, an entire month. We made these arrangements a year ago under the assumption that the worldwide financial infrastructure wouldn't totally collapse. Our bad.

We rented a condo in Wailea, Maui, above a golf course with a breathtaking view of the ocean and the Wailea shopping mall. I figured, why stay at one of those fancy luxury hotels when we can just partake in the facilities of all of them? It's as if "the Wedding Crashers" went along on the honeymoons too.

The unit was lovely. These complexes all have cute names like *Ekolu Terrace*. We stayed at the *E-coli Village*.

At various times we were also joined by Matt (the Apple Design Engineer of our eye) and Annie (Dorothy Parker without the psychotic episodes).

Spent most of our time at the Grand Wailea. This is a true luxury resort but HUGE. It should be called the MGM Grand Wailea. Picture a combination of the Bellagio and Disney's Blizzard Beach Water Slide Park. Lagoons, spas, thirty million dollars in sculptures that no one notices and are primarily used as jungle gyms by kids, its own chapel (tan with Jesus), and exclusive shops with prices so staggeringly high that even rappers don't buy their jewelry.

Another exclusive feature is their Grand Spa where a massage is just part of the package. Unfortunately the other part is not a "happy ending." It's an absurd beginning. You're invited to go through a series of kelp baths, loofah sponge baths (administered by a guy named Thor), sea salt exfoliation treatment, and a Japanese Furo bath. You're then offered a selection of massages. My favorite: they pour hot oil on your forehead. All this for only five times what a normal massage would cost (*with* a happy ending). Plus, there is a handout on "spa etiquette." Among the entries: "ladies on their menstrual cycle are asked not to utilize the Terme." That's actually good advice for anywhere.

The hotel's thatched hut tropical lagoon restaurant is actually named Humuhumunukunukuapua's. Annie says when she goes on *Survivor* that's going to be her tribe's name.

Cabana prices have gone up to $200 a day. The most expensive shade in Hawaii. And you can make reservations a year in advance. For only $100 you can reserve cloud cover.

A tourist was bitten by a shark 200 yards from our beach. So all beaches along the immediate coast were closed for a day…except the one that fronts the Four Seasons. Guess they figured with all the Hollywood agents there no shark would ever attack – professional courtesy.

You can't walk ten feet in any direction without some jogger calling out "*on your left*!"

Every time I return to Hawaii I am more convinced it's the most spectacular place on earth.

Imagine the beauty of *Lost* without the polar bears, mysterious smoke monsters, the "Others," abductions, explosions, killer force fields, flying spears, illegal medical experiments, and that annoying couple they buried alive.

Do you like great pizza? Then go to Hawaii. Matteo's on Maui. The reverse is not true. You can't go to Italy for scrumptious poi.

Even in paradise there are people with deep-rooted psychological problems. Hence the "*Therapy Sports Grille.*" A few Mai Tai's and Pac 10 basketball and Hawaiians are back on the road to mental wellness.

You can't help but reflect on December 7th, especially if you're in Hawaii. When our kids were little we took them on the U.S.S. Arizona tour. Annie pretty much summed it up. "You look down, you feel sad, you go." I would only add: "You remember."

I know this is an awkward transition but you MUST try Sansei in Kihei for the greatest sushi this side of our former enemies.

Saw an ambulance roaring through south Maui, lights on, siren blazing – toting a boat. It is not a good idea to need emergency medical care during whale watching season.

During one of the many beautiful weddings at the Grand Wailea's too-cute-for-words chapel, the gorgeous bride walked down the aisle, heard the organ music, the applause from her beloved friends and family, and a guy yelling "*on your left*!"

The only reason Hawaii wants to stay in the union is so they'll be eligible for the next *American Idol.*

Barack Obama/Abe Lincoln similarities is a current hot topic. And why not? Both were raised in Hawaii. Both look good in shorts.

This is not a big selling point to me: *Alex Air -the only DOORS OFF helicopter tour company on Maui.*

One of the many great things about this paradise – you never hear Paul McCartney's inane "Having a Wonderful Christmas" on the radio. Instead they play Paul Anka's "Christmas in Japan."

Although McCartney *was* represented. At the art gallery in the next door high end fashion mall a big sign boasts an exhibition of paintings from Paul McCartney, Tony Bennett...and then in much smaller letters, Picasso.

The Aloha Spirit is alive: Supposedly Maui police have shot more civilians than all other Hawaiian island police forces combined. "Book him, Dan -" BANG!!!

Did not get to Hana. The only way in is through a treacherous road that zigzags over 56 one-lane bridges and snakes around more than 617 hairpin turns. If God Himself greeted you at City Hall with a lei I wouldn't make that drive.

Nor did I see the sunrise at Haleakala. But did get a report from someone who did. A bus picks you up 2:30 in the morning. You drive an hour and a half to the top of this massive shield volcano. By top I mean 10,023 feet. You get out in your shorts, flip flops, and aloha shirt – it's pitch black, and 22 degrees (literally). When the sun comes up (two hours later) it will rise to 37. Finally the dawn. It's breathtaking, awesome, and your teeth are chattering like castanets. You don't want to even *think* about the possibility that there's a YouTube video of this. You get on the bus and either go home or into shock.

For more fun you can bike down the outside of the volcano... like a rocket on a two-lane winding road that hugs a cliff that's steeper than those in Road Runner cartoons. Bikers must also negotiate tour buses, vans, and tourists in unfamiliar rental cars. In 2007 there were three biker fatalities. Bike tours (when they're not suspended) are $100 - $150 dollars. Bring a parachute.

But we did visit quaint Lahaina. Strolled past the charming Crazy-T-Shirt and souvenir soap stores. This bawdy whaling port has not changed in a hundred years.

Lahaina also features one of the largest banyan trees in the United

States. So a big attraction is shade.

For all the hoopla of Lahaina, we found quite a few other smaller, lesser-known little towns that were far more charming and KFC-free. Paia, for one (Paia of course is the birthplace of Abe Lincoln). It's advertised as a throwback "hippie" village. And I must say it took me right back to the '60s when hippies supported their drug habits by selling gelato.

Makawao is another quaint attraction. Up country, it's a little cowboy town, specializing in glass blowing – just like Wyatt Earp and Billy the Kid used to do. I kept looking for the jail and saloon but alas they've given way to art galleries and a market that makes fresh donuts. But get there early. They go fast. There's usually a shoot-out in the town square for the last cruller.

There's no longer a sheriff, but Makawao does have two hypnotherapists and a certified colon specialist.

Every restaurant in Hawaii serves ribs. Even the vegan ones. I bet that colon specialist does a bang-up business.

James A. Michener was inspired to write *Hawaii* on the islands. My daughter, Annie worked on her spec *Big Bang Theory*.

I wonder how many vacationers think "*wi-fi*" is a Hawaiian word.

Went to Spago's at the Four Season with writer friends Howard & Karen. We let the kids fend for themselves. A half-hour into dinner I get a call from Annie. "Hey, Dad, turn around. Look to your left." My first thought was "what the fuck are they doing at Spago? This is going to cost me a fortune!" My second was "where are they?" I told Annie I didn't see them. She said, "more to your left. We're waving." I still couldn't see them. Now I'm getting panicky. Jesus, am I going blind? This went on for two more minutes. Finally she said, "We're at CPK, have a nice dinner," they laughed and hung up. I love my children but they're evil.

Every lounge singer on Maui thinks she's Norah Jones. I miss the days when they all thought they were Joni Mitchell.

Classiest store title in Maui: "Who Cut the Cheese?" I just feel bad for the coffee shop right next door.

Attention criminals! Stay out of the Foodland shopping center! Right between the Rainbow Attic and Aroma's Italian restaurant is the Kehei police department. My guess is all three close at 10.

Do not miss Mama's Fish House. Spectacular cuisine. Frank

Sinatra, Aerosmith, and Abe Lincoln have eaten there so you *know* it's good. Also try the General Store in Hali'imaile. It's the best middle-of-nowhere restaurant you'll ever (hopefully) find. The sashimi napoleon is orgasmic!

Maui onions cost more on Maui than in Los Angeles.

On the other hand, you get some pretty good deals on wine at Longs Drugs.

Sugar In The Raw packets: sugar from Hawaii, packaged in Brooklyn.

Spotted on the side of a van: SURF LESSONS – WE SPECIAL-IZE IN BEGINNERS AND COWARDS

At night there's not a lot to do but rent movies. There are a lot more direct-to-video releases at Blockbuster than I remember. How these gems never get major distribution deals I'll never know. (Note: these are *actual* titles and taglines.) *Father Of The Kamika* – "Official Selection 1974 Geijyutsusa Arts Festival," *Ninja Cheerleaders* – "Fight to Cheer Another Day," *Pirates Of The Salt Lakes* – "Pirate Talk so Salty, You Won't Believe Your Buccaneers" (get it?), *Zombie Strippers* – "They'll Dance for a Fee, But Devour You for Free." *What Would Jesus Buy?* – "The Movie that Santa Doesn't Want You to See." And finally… *Kenny*. My namesake is a guy who cleans toilets. The tagline: "He's Number One with Your Number Two." Oh well. At least one reviewer called it "The Citizen Kane of Romantic Comedies About Sewage."

Of all the times we've been to Hawaii, believe it or not, we've never been to an authentic Marriott Hotel Luau. Until now.

First we adhered to ancient Hawaiian tradition by having tropical drinks on the Astroturf surface and checking out all the merchants selling cheap jewelry and wooden tikis. Then we wandered down to the oceanfront to watch the sunset while people took our pictures and told us where we could buy them.

The kalua pig with an apple in its mouth was removed from the spit, I guess (I was at the bar having the first of many pina coladas) and it was royal feast time. The macaroni salad was to die from. Had poi for the first time. Poi is Hawaiian for "Wallpaper Paste."

Meanwhile, a Hawaiian combo played Island favorites like (I kid you not) "The Brady Bunch Theme" and Aerosmith's "Dream On."

The big show began, filled with dancers in elaborate costumes.

Instead of junk jewelry they should have been selling those coconut bras the hula dancers were wearing. Those were stylin'! The hula girls were gorgeous and the hula guys were buff and beautiful, and when they're not doing luaus they're probably letting girls lick Reddi Whip off their chests at bachelorette parties.

The theme of the show was the story of Hawaii, circa the 11th Century. I was thrown a little in one scene when one of the hula girls had a cell phone.

The dances, pageantry, and legend continued, and I can honestly say that anyone who had two or more drinks was saying, "What the fuck??" After three drinks Annie said to her daddy, "You're cut off!"

The finale was truly spectacular though. Fire dancers. One in particular was amazing – twirling two flaming batons. You always wonder – how do majorettes ever make money? Well, the key is talent and a lighter.

The show ended to much applause and the traditional chants of "Aloha" and "Don't forget to get your souvenir photos!"

Okay, now we've done that. Next trip maybe the Virgin Sacrifice at the Sheraton.

I can't believe how fast the month sped by. Only two days of heavy rain, three of hurricane-like wind, no statewide power outages, a mere 47 bug bites, and I only got sick once (whale retching). But I am left with cherished memories and from now on every time I see a penny or a five-dollar bill I will automatically think of Hawaii.

PHOENIX

March 2009

THIS TRAVELOGUE IS A combination of three trips to Phoenix I made this month to cover the Dodgers' spring training.

This is a sprawling city of giant shopping malls broken up by sports complexes. Oh, and numerous aircraft bone yards. From rusted out WWII planes to 747s that haven't flown since Braniff went under, they're all here. Was hoping to swing by and pick up an L1011 fuselage but time got away.

Other major attractions Phoenix can boast about: the world's largest Kachina Doll, the world's largest inflatable dam, and the world's largest sneezing nose – a fitting tribute to the many allergies people suffer from in these parts.

Famous sons of the Valley of the Sun include Steven Spielberg, retired golfer Alice Cooper, Wonder Woman, Hugh Downs, Barry Goldwater, and most prominent of them all – *American Idol*, Jordin Sparks.

To get anywhere in Phoenix – to work, a restaurant, the rental car outpost from the airport – you just get on the freeway and go 13.2 miles. Everything is 13.2 miles away. Except Circle K's. There are two on every corner. How much beef jerky can this town chew?

I've seen ads for the University of Phoenix in Los Angeles, St. Louis, and Philadelphia but who knew? They also have a branch in Phoenix!

On my first trip I stayed at a Holiday Inn Express near the big University of Phoenix stadium, (home of the Super Bowl losing Cardinals) which looks like an enormous Jiffy Pop bag just before it explodes. What college has an enormous stadium but no football team? And no campus even!

You can sure feel the effects of the economy. The Dodgers kicked off the Cactus League season against the Cubs in Mesa. Usually Cubs tickets are harder to get in the desert than oceanfront property but this year even opening day didn't sell out. Obama's bailout plan is going to have to include scalpers I'm afraid.

Next day we headed to Scottsdale (13.2 miles) to face the dreaded Giants. Scottsdale is the ritzy section of Phoenix. As you approach it the car dealerships get much more upscale.

Scottsdale is gorgeous. Known for its swank resorts, golf courses, art galleries (you better like *southwestern*), and the Bob Crane murder.

Most restaurants in Phoenix are a chain, but at least in Scottsdale they're Morton's and Roy's. Most everywhere else they're McDonald's and Roy Rogers.

But it was not worth driving 13.2 miles for fine dining when right nearby there was a Tilted Kilts. Who knew anyone could improve on Hooters? The breasts seemed more real, the kilts more skimpy. And for an even finer culinary experience, I recommend the chicken wings appetizer. When they arrive ask for a different dipping sauce so the hot tattooed Betty Boop has to return and lean over your table to deliver it. Any master chef will tell you – it's all in the presentation.

The new Dodger complex in Glendale is magnificent! Camelback Ranch (not to be confused with the Mustang Ranch – the other spring training destination for most men). Camelback Ranch looks like it was designed by Frank Lloyd Wright after a long night at Tilted Kilts.

Missed the big ostrich festival. Ostrich races AND Foghat!!!

Best Phoenix TV show bar none is *Lone Butte Casino's Lucky Break* every Saturday night at 10:30 on channel 5. It's a cheesy *American Idol* rip-off hosted by Olympic Gold medal swimmer, Amy Van Dyken. Grand prize is a dinner for two at the Verona Chop House. One of the judges is a plumber. I'm not making this up! One of the contestants was 83 and just had a hip replacement. Did not bust a lot of moves in her routine. Halfway through, the judges blasted an air horn to stop her. She didn't hear it. Eventually she had to be helped off the stage. Next up was her daughter who got the air horn even sooner. Five contestants ended in a tie so to break it they each had to sing "Happy Birthday." One actually stumbled over the words. She won.

Come ye all to the annual Arizona Renaissance Fair. Wear ye heavy garb of velvet and wool or ye full suit of armor. Imagine if they held this in August. Merry Old England during the Bubonic Plague.

You can go Indoor Skydiving in Phoenix. A simulated freefall chamber will drop you 13,000 feet at 120 mph. It seems to me skydiving (outdoors) requires courage but offers an incomparable thrill. Indoor skydiving down an elevator shaft requires losing a bet at a frat party.

Pheeniks is number nine on the US list of most misspelled cities.

I was really stylin' the second trip. My rental car was a maroon Chevy hearse. At least that's what it looked like. I kept checking to make sure Bob Crane wasn't in the back.

Alas, spring training is over. Last week rooms at the Holiday Inn Express were $165 a night. This week they're free with a ticket stub from the Ostrich races. But if you're a baseball fan or you just want to see if the Red Lobster in Phoenix is any different from the one in your town, you've got to come to Arizona in March. I'll never be able to see *Hogan's Heroes* again without wanting to go back.

DISNEYLAND/CALIFORNIA ADVENTURE

May 2009

DEBBY AND I WENT to Disneyland. Since becoming an adult this was the first time I was ever there without kids or a joint. No strollers, no giant diaper bags, no getting home and realizing we had left somebody. Also, we had never seen the adjacent California Adventure and wanted to go before it eventually shuts down or is completely rethought.

We figured: go before the summer begins and kids are out of school. I guess that now means February. Disneyland was packed. There were lines for everything. The biggest: Indiana Jones and the Temple of Waiting, Space Mountain, and churros. The Small World attraction is closed for renovation (thank God). A big fence surrounds it. So the line was only a half an hour.

I wore a golf shirt and long pants. I was waaaay overdressed. Come on, people! At least the ratty t-shirts and torn plaid shorts should *fit*! You're going to be taking pictures in those rags.

As always, the park was immaculate… although I could swear one of the 60-year-old maintenance men in an elf suit was a former producer of *Taxi*. And the teenagers who work there remain the nicest, perkiest, *helpfulliest* David Archuleta and Carrie Underwood clones you could find this side of Stepford.

I'm guessing the teens with major imperfections like acne or no dimples are assigned to wear those bulky heavy character costumes. It was 90 degrees and Winnie the Pooh was staggering around, tripping over strollers, kicking little tykes; occasionally sticking his head in an ice cream pushcart for relief.

Happy to say that the new Pirates of the Caribbean ride wasn't ruined by the improvements. There were a few Jack Sparrows added and a nifty Davy Jones hologram, but otherwise it's pretty much the same. Oh maybe a little less raping, but the spirit of fun is still there.

To avoid standing in endless lines Disneyland now offers "Fast

Passes" for most major rides. It allows you to return for wait-free boarding. We got our Fast Passes for Space Mountain at 1:00 PM. Our reservations were for 9:30, thus saving us fifteen minutes had we stood in the normal line.

I was a good boy this trip. I did not stand up and ask Mr. Lincoln a question, nor did I buy a Mouseketeer hat, have them scroll "*Vincent*" then rip off one of the ears.

With all the spectacular photo-ops Disneyland provides, all day long I saw people taking pictures of each other while standing in lines. We are truly a country of idiots.

Then there are the women trying to walk all day and night in ankle strap wedges. And they wonder why they're crippled by Fantasyland.

Gas prices are so high that the Autopia cars are now just being pushed by Disney employees.

The irony of the Indiana Jones ride is that Harrison Ford probably can no longer ride it. It's way too violent and rugged for a 66-year-old man.

We moved over to California Adventure, which is like going from Times Square on New Year's Eve to downtown Flint, Michigan a year after they closed the GM plant.

The only thing worth seeing is "Soarin' Over California." It's a simulated hang glide tour over the state. If only I could simulate flying on American Airlines instead of actually *having* to fly on American Airlines.

Wandered around the park. Don't know the names of the "lands" per se but there's one that's kind of rustic, which my wife just called "*Wilderness Shit*." They pipe in this real stirring John Williams type music and I must say, coming out of the restroom I thought, "There've been times in my life when I could have really used this."

Next we encountered a beach boardwalk-themed land. The John Williams music gave way to Beach Boys tunes on a calliope. All these years I never knew that "God Only Knows" was a circus song.

Disney – the company that brought you *Song of the South* and tar babies now presents "Pizza Oom Mow Mow" on the pier at California Adventure.

There's a big classic Coney Island style rollercoaster and something called the "Twilight Zone Tower of Terror." Not wanting my first major stroke to be in a place where the paramedics all wear Peter

Pan costumes, I passed on both.

We returned to Disneyland, nostalgic for the days when California Adventure was still a parking lot.

Night fell on the Magic Kingdom and it got a little chilly. No worries. There's a clothing store every hundred feet. Me: "Excuse me, Tracy/Stacey/Kaysee/Lacy, do you have a men's sweatshirt that doesn't have Tinkerbell on it? Or Mickey in a wizard's cap? Or Mulan? Or a fucking fairy castle!?" I bought a Davy Crockett coonskin cap so at least my head was warm.

The Haunted Mansion is now inhabited by a bilingual ghost. He gives spooky instructions in both English and Spanish.

Never got to Toontown. There were enough over-stimulated, sugar revved, screaming, out-of-control little hellions in all the other lands.

And I always wonder – how many of these children were conceived on Tom Sawyer's Island during Grad Night?

Following the fireworks and "Disney Dwarfs on Parade" or whatever the hell that noisy thing was, we dutifully reported to Space Mountain to take advantage of our Fast Pass. Wow! Space Mountain was always great but this new revamped version is awesome. You know they mean business when they tell you to take your glasses off. As I was crawling off the rocket sled on my hands and knees I said to my wife, "Now THAT'S a thrill ride!"

Finally, it was time to leave. Where did twelve hours and hundreds of dollars go? A half hour to catch the tram and another half hour to find our car in the parking structure the size of Liechtenstein, and we were merrily on our way to hit massive traffic on the Santa Ana freeway at midnight.

I have always loved Disneyland. I'm not ashamed to say it. I am ashamed to wear any of those sweatshirts but even as a five year-old curmudgeon I marveled at the imagination, scope, and vision of this wondrous (albeit highly profitable) world. So I will be back. Soon. My Fast Pass reservation for the Little Nemo Submarine Voyage is November 21st at 6:30 AM.

SAN DIEGO/NEW YORK/ MILWAUKEE

July 2009

NO ONE GOES FROM San Diego to New York to Milwaukee unless they're running from authorities or on a road trip with the Los Angeles Dodgers.

San Diego has really been built up over the last few years. More Radio Shacks and Targets in the 'burbs and a huge renovation project downtown where the Gas Lamp District has become a late night restaurant and bar Mecca. This is not the sleepy provincial San Diego I used to know. Last call is now 11:15!

A big reason for the Gas Lamp renaissance: Petco Park, the new downtown home of the San Diego Padres. Folks now have something else to see in the district besides drunken sailors urinating.

Petco Park is one of those "new with a nod to the old" ballparks. The four-story brick Western Metal Supply Company warehouse remains wedged down the left field line. Also intact from the original 1909 design are the twelve party suites that were a big part of the Western Metal Supply Company. The outfield dimensions are wacky. There's like a little jury box that juts out in right field. On one hand you could say it gives the ballpark character. On the other you could say, "Why???"

There's a statue across the street of former Padre, Tony Gwynn, one of the two greatest citizens to ever come out of San Diego (the mascot Chicken being the other).

One concession to the modern era is the ballpark signage that is everywhere. I'm surprised the first and third base coaches aren't obligated to wear sandwich boards. The facades of every level are covered with neon ads. In left field there is one for "*Bimbo Bimbo.*" I suspect that section is reserved for the players' first wives.

The Padres still have Hall-of-Famer Jerry Coleman behind the mic. The Colonel is now 84, God bless him. Jerry is famous for classic malaprops. When I broadcast Padres games with him in the mid

'90s he delivered my favorite. "There's a fly ball to center... foul!"

It was the 4th of July weekend and firework shows were everywhere. I watched one from the broadcast booth at Petco Park while on the air. It was like hosting Dodger Talk during the Dresden bombings.

A number of communities had fairs and festivals for the 4th. Many featured circus workshops, which makes sense considering the increase in San Diego traffic. Now when locals carpool they can get thirty in a Kia.

Speaking of the circus, Manny Ramirez – lovable baseball drug policy abuser and hitting idiot savant – returned from his 50-game suspension. This caused a media frenzy the likes of which hadn't been seen since the Farrah Fawcett funeral three days earlier.

Missed the San Diego County Fair. Was hoping to enter the watermelon seed spitting contest (soon to become an Olympic event), worm racing, the frozen t-shirt contest (whatever the hell that is), most patriotic costume competition (I even had my "Daughter of the Revolution" dress packed), "Kazoo that Tune," and what old fashion county fair would be complete without the traditional "Cell phone Texting Contest?"

The Chargers are the only NFL team that did not sell out their home opener. Make no mistake, San Diego is a big league sports town. But the sport is Boogie Boarding.

A Fischer-Price "Loving Family Dollhouse" in La Jolla now goes for a million-five.

Had the ballplayers known there was a nude beach in La Jolla (Black's) a group of them might have gone there rather than Legoland. I skipped it as well. Once you reach 30, Black's Beach is the *Gentleman's Club of the Truly Pathetic.*

Sunday was getaway day. An afternoon game with the Padres then an evening flight to New York. The Dodgers blew a five run lead in the ninth, but finally won it in the 13th. Time of game: a brisk four hours and thirty-three minutes. We staggered into our New York hotel at 3:45 AM.

That hotel was the Le Parker Meridien, which is a huge upgrade from the Grand Central Hyatt – location of other teams and Columbian drug dealers. Le Parker Meridien is very chic. It's the first choice of Eurotrash. The décor is a cross between Art Deco and the Jetsons. It provides sophistication and class for the discerning guest and cartoons in the elevator for Manny Ramirez.

New York was glorious! Perfect weather! You know you're getting close to Central Park when you're accosted by five people on every corner wanting to rent you a bicycle, sign you up for a bus tour, or sell you half price tickets to *Naked Boys Singing*.

There's a street vendor on Madison Avenue who hands out business cards. Call "Cheikh" anytime for bags, scarves, and jewelry. His card table is located at 77th Street & Madison Avenue… unless it rains or he's run off.

The Mets now play in their $800,000,000 new home, Citi Field (although it should be called "Taxpayers' Field"). What a vast improvement over Shea Stadium, where every tunnel was a sewer. Citi Field has all the amenities of modern stadiums along with seats so close to the action you could get clocked by a flying bat. But its most impressive feature is a huge rotunda celebrating Jackie Robinson. So, between that and the exterior, which is a nod to old Ebbetts Field in Brooklyn, the ballpark is pretty much an ode to the Dodgers. That's fine for me, but the Mets have a rich history themselves and I wish more of that were on display. Where's a statue of Choo Choo Coleman?

Most new ballparks have gleaming adjacent concourses where fans can spill out into restaurants, bars, and souvenir arcades. At Citi Field you have your choice of muffler stores, repair garages, and auto body and paint shops. Usually the teams get a cut of the action, but in this case I suspect the Sopranos got there first.

That nice weather I mentioned ended Tuesday just as a group of us piled into a town car at midnight to leave the park. I wanted to stay longer and browse for fuel pumps but was overruled. So we headed back to the city right when a tornado hit Yonkers. (Since when did New York become friggin' Kansas?) The sky opened up and we were deluged with rain. Add to that, construction work near the 59th Street Bridge and we were living *Bonfire of the Vanities* during a monsoon. And picture Mel Gibson from *Lethal Weapon* as the driver… with Jews in the car.

"Manny Mania" continued. The New York press converged on him like a Tootsie Roll at a fat farm. He agreed to not answer the same questions he didn't answer in San Diego.

From Gotham, it was a late night flight to Milwaukee where we stayed at the historic Pfister. The Pfister is pfirst class. It's an old regal downtown hotel that just happens to be haunted. Some ballplayers are so freaked they stay elsewhere, or sleep holding a bat for protection. Carlos Gomez of the Twins was getting out of the shower and his iPod suddenly went haywire, so instead of calling AppleCare (or Ghostbusters?), he raced out to the lobby without his pants. I shared a room with the Ghost of Christmas Future. He told me that "*UFC Undisputed*" will sell out quick this season so shop early.

One thing I've discovered about Milwaukee – it's in a time warp. The buildings, the cars, the people – it's 1956. Friday night's postgame concert featured newcomers Buddy Holly and the Crickets. In an attempt to blend in I wore an "*Adlai Stevenson for President*" button.

Missed the 60th annual *South Shore Frolic*. Friday's big attraction for the kiddies: a chainsaw artist. And if that's your cup of tea, visit the Ambrosia Chocolate Factory where Jeffrey Dahmer was a trusted employee.

I did, however, get out to Karl Ratzsch's for the best German food this side of Stalag 13. Order anything with a "Z" in its name.

Miller Park, home of the Brewers, boasts a retractable roof (handy since it snows 300 days a year), cheerleaders, a giant slide where mascot Bernie Brewer plunges into suds throughout the game, racing seven foot frankfurters, and national treasure, Bob Uecker (their long-time radio voice).

The retractable roof can be problematic. One sweltering summer day they closed it during a game because thundershowers loomed. But, the result was they trapped the heat and humidity IN the ballpark. Someone said that when the fat lady finally did sing she was a size four.

Miller also has something no other ballpark in the land can match -- the world's greatest bratwursts. That comes as no surprise, certainly, this is Germantown, but they're even better than expected. One bite and you can actually feel an artery clog up. Yet, it's so good you finish it anyway. The record for most bratwursts consumed here in one day is seventeen by a gentleman from Menomonee Falls. From what I understand, he's buried somewhere down the left-field line. The condiments for these brats consist of the usual mustard-onion-relish fare, along with sauerkraut, and something they call "Secret Stadium

Sauce." Nobody will divulge just what is in this thick red secret goo, but it was allegedly discovered during an early experiment of the Manhattan Project.

And then there are the tailgate parties. Folks here jam the parking lots long before game time and crack out the barbeques and coolers, filling the air with heavenly aromas and grease. If you love block parties with total strangers, whose only common bond is the mass consumption of life-endangering substances, you've gotta love Milwaukee. I, of course, do.

One more thing – the Ghost of Christmas Future also wants to remind you to use zip codes when sending packages through the mail. Thank you.

DENVER/CINCINNATI

August 2009

ON THE ROAD AGAIN with the Dodgers. This time Denver and Cincinnati – two cities that are incredibly similar in that neither is near an ocean. The most absurd moment happened before we even boarded the plane in Los Angeles. An overzealous TSA agent was patting down Vin Scully. Yeah, it's common knowledge terrorists like to hide explosives in World Series rings.

Stayed at the Ritz-Carlton hotel downtown (or, as they call it – "LoDo"). I had a beautifully appointed room with a spectacular view of the Greyhound Bus Terminal. (How convenient for all the bus travelers that there is a Ritz-Carlton across the street so they have somewhere to crash before moving on to Utah).

Was walking distance to the 16th Street Mall, where red oak trees and fountains line this showpiece featuring a thousand Verizon and AT&T stores and great local dining from Chili's to The Cheesecake Factory.

Also walking distance is the ballpark, Coors Field. It's a Camden Yards clone combining modern conveniences (luxury boxes, stadium clubs, lights) and retro features (brick exterior, and uh… brick exterior). But because of the thin air, baseballs travel farther there. So to compensate they moved the fences back to where they're now beyond the horizon.

John Elway is to Denver what Andy Taylor is to Mayberry and Jesus Christ is to Rome.

Nearby is Red Rocks, an outdoor amphitheater cut into a mountain. It's a breathtaking setting. If John Denver were still alive this is where he'd be playing every week, sharing the bill with Harry Chapin if he were still alive. Red Rocks also has the distinction of being the only U.S. venue in which the Beatles did not sell out.

There is new meaning to "Rocky Mountain High." Authorities have seized nearly 20,000 marijuana plants from Colorado national forests. It's bad enough rangers have to deal with bears stealing pic-i-nic baskets, now they have to contend with international drug cartels.

I bet if those plants were there in the '60s that Beatles concert would have sold out in eleven minutes.

Denver is the most sexually active city in America. Contraceptive sales are 189% higher within the city limits than the national average (sales of female contraceptives are a whopping 278% higher). Coincidentally, Denver also has the world's largest brewery (Coors).

And easily the best, most dramatic thunderstorms! Huge bolts of lightening create a thrilling panorama, and what better place to view them than from a radio booth at a baseball stadium surrounded by electronic equipment and light towers?

There is now only one newspaper in town, *The Post*. *The Rocky Mountain News* (my favorite of the two because it once gave *Almost Perfect* a decent review) folded in February after 150 years of service. This is now an all-too-familiar scenario in most major cities. Did Al Gore have any idea of this when he invented the internet?

If you're driving from "LoDo" to the I-70 with kids and you're looking for a fun thing for them to do, have them count the number of gun shops they see along the way. The kinder will be occupied the entire trip!

You gotta love the name of Denver's mayor – Hizzonor John Wright Hickenlooper.

Things not to miss: The Butterfly Pavilion insect zoo, the "Mind Eraser" rollercoaster at Elitch Gardens, the giant cement slide at Bear Valley Park that looks like a vagina, the Buckhorn Exchange restaurant with 500 stuffed animals (it's how I imagine Elizabeth Hasselbeck's bedroom), the stone marker that claims to be the birthplace of the cheeseburger, and any CVS pharmacy for contraceptives.

The Dodgers won two out of three and we beat a hasty retreat to the Queen City.

All you really need to know about Cincinnati, Ohio is that Jerry Springer was their former mayor.

Across the Ohio River is Kentucky. It's the dividing line between the North and South. In Cincinnati you can't smoke in restaurants. In Kentucky it's encouraged, as is smoking in church, day care centers, and ICU's.

Stayed across the street from Fountain Square. It's what you see in the opening titles of *WKRP In Cincinnati*. The centerpiece is the Tyler Davidson Fountain – actually *more* center now that they moved it a few feet. Yes, it cost $42,000,000 to accomplish that, but it's much easier to frame up in your cell phone camera now!

Cincinnati proudly calls itself *Porkopolis*. The pork industry has always been major there. A few years ago they had a public arts project called "The Big Pig Gig" in which more than 400 brightly painted ceramic pigs were displayed all over town. Some had names like "Six Degrees of Kevin Bacon."

Caught the Quacky Races at Fountain Square. Teams in ridiculous duck costumes battled a rigorous obstacle course to win... I dunno, something (maybe the chance to compete on *I Survived A Japanese Game Show*). This is in anticipation of the big event - "The Rubber Duck Regatta" where they dump 100,000 rubber duckys into the Ohio River and let them race for a quarter mile of thrills. People buy the ducks and the proceeds go to charity. At least it's not 100,000 pigs.

Saturday, I was really privileged to attend the Cornhole Championships at Fountain Square. It turns out cornholing is also a game. Who knew? You play it with a board and bags and it was originated in Cincinnati. Still, how do you tell a girl you're hoping to get into the sack that you're a champion cornholer?

Graeter's Ice Cream is a must! Homemade, by hand, delicious. A member of our traveling party bought 12 pints. I hope he planned to ship them home and not finish them all in his room because he's sad.

On the other hand, Skyline Chili is highly overrated. It's not even chili. It's runny meat on spaghetti with a disgusting dollop of cheese on top. I'm sure Skyline Chili has caused more clogged arteries and prison riots than any other regional delicacy in the world.

The Reds play in the "Great American Ballpark." Locals call it the "Pretty Good American Ballpark" and ballplayers call it "the Great American Smallpark" - it is very hitter friendly. From the two upper decks you get a nice view of Kentucky (although it's usually obscured in a cloud of smoke), and 100,000 rubber ducks.

My favorite ballpark ad: "1-800-GOT-JUNK: THE OFFICIAL REMOVAL SERVICE OF THE CINCINNATI REDS."

Several readers of my blog came out to the game on Saturday just to meet me! Aw, who'm I kidding? They were there for "Reusable Grocery Bag Day."

If you like ribs, go to Montgomery's. Bob Hope used to have them shipped to him. That's high praise until you realize the alternative was

Army chow in Da Nang.

About nine blocks from the ballpark is an area known as "Over-the-Rhine." It's rated the single most dangerous neighborhood in the country! And remember, cornholing is legal. "Over-the-Rhine's" crime rate is higher per capita than any other U.S. neighborhood. So take that Detroit, New York, and Phoenix! It's so out of control people are even smoking in restaurants! Police raided a home just last week and confiscated 400 brightly painted ceramic pigs!

"Dem Bums" took two out of three from the Reds and we headed home still in first place. And even better – no Dodger is out for the rest of the year after eating a bowl of Skyline Chili.

I guess the most appropriate way to say goodbye from Cincinnati is "*Abadee, abadee, abadee, th-th-that's all folks!*"

ST. LOUIS

October 2009

TOOK A QUICK TRIP to St. Louis with the Dodgers this weekend. Long enough to eliminate the Cardinals and move on to the National League Championship Series. However, on the bus to the airport, we passed the Edward Jones Dome – a gentle reminder that Los Angeles may have beaten the Red Birds, but St. Louis still has our Rams.

St. Loo is famous of course for the Anheuser-Busch brewery. Although, locals insist it's not the same now that the Busch family has sold it to Germans. They claim the beer tastes different. I couldn't tell, but I did notice the Clydesdales goose-stepping in a recent parade.

St. Louis in the fall is highly preferable to St. Louis in the spring (when there are floods), the winter (when there are blizzards), and the summer (when it is so hot and humid it's like living in Shaquille O'Neal's gym shoes). The leaves were beginning to change, there was a crispness in the air, and late day shadows from the Budweiser billboards blanketed much of the city.

The signature Gateway Arch stands tall and shimmers, still awaiting a companion arch so that the world's first ten story McDonald's can open.

Nearby is the Citygarden with a giant statue of Pinocchio. Why, I don't know. Maybe it's a monument to liars. If so, it should be in Washington.

St. Louis is the birthplace of Chuck Berry, owner of many hit and police records. It's also the "Home of the Blues." Several cities claim to be the "Home of the Blues" but so what? George Clooney has eighteen homes. Why can't the Blues have six?

Mark Twain was raised in nearby Hannibal. For more information about Hannibal call 1-TOM-AND-HUCK.

Sports and Budweiser are very big here (no matter how it tastes). And there are some great restaurant/sports bars. Mike Shannon's. Jbuck's. Every major figure associated with the Cardinals other than Jose Oquendo has his own eat-and-drinkery. The pulled pork sandwich at Jbuck's is delish.

I tried to get some of the players to join me for a day at Sophia M. Sach's Butterfly House, but they passed. To their credit, they could have lied and said they needed to prepare for the most important game of the season, but instead they just said, "No fucking way, Mary!" It's taken me two years to earn that kind of respect.

There are quite a few casinos on the Mississippi River. They used to be on riverboats. Now they're inland as far as the airport. A lot of Dodger per diem is currently in their hands. Some of these casinos are open 24 hours…

… as is Steak & Shake. There must be a thousand of these in the area. I don't know about you, but when I get a little hungry at 4:00 in the morning, nothing satisfies my craving like a good T-Bone with a vanilla shake.

Saw an ad for Pulaski County that boasted "Home of Fort Leonard Wood." This is an attraction??? An army base in the middle of the Ozarks, out where Lil' Abner and Mammy Yokum lives? Leonard Wood (known affectionately as "Little Korea" in the winter) is hailed in the ad as - "The Perfect Setting For a Family Getaway." Yeah, maybe for Oliver North's family.

On one of these jaunts to the "Show Me State", I've got to get to Branson. This is the town where entertainers go to die… twice a night. Theater after theater offer such acts as Andy Williams, Jim Stafford (his big hit "Spiders & Snakes" changed the face of popular music forever!), the great Yakov Smirnoff (his ad says, "You'll laugh your YAK OFF!"), Paul Revere & the Raiders (good luck getting into those red velvet suits you wore in 1966), Amazing Pets, the Country & Hobo Show, and a Neil Diamond tribute ("You'll experience the *feel* of Neil Diamond.").

To the business at hand, the Dodgers were there to face the Cardinals in the National League Division Series. The winner becomes the champion of, well… nothing. But they get to go on to the next round. The Dodgers came in needing only one more win.

The Cards play in the new Busch Stadium, just a stone's throw from the old Busch Stadium. It's in a perfect downtown location, right near the former home of the Museum of Bowling (not enough people signed up for their ten week course on "how to score.") and the Tums factory. Beyond centerfield you can see the Arch and the Old

Courthouse. Fans pack the park and all wear red. It's quite a sight. Except in April and September (when it's freezing), and June, July and August (when it's unbearably hot), I love going to baseball games in St. Louis.

No one will ever take the great Vin Scully's chair, but I at least got to sit in it for a few moments. I hosted pre and post game Dodger Talk from the spot Vin occupied. No joke – it was one of the highlights of my life.

The Dodgers won and it was only fitting that along with the champagne, they poured Budweiser beer all over each other. And me. I walked back to the hotel smelling like Kiefer Sutherland at any given 2:00 AM.

My heart kind of goes out to the fine folks of St. Louis. Winter is coming, their beloved Cardinals were eliminated, and Rush Limbaugh now wants to buy the Rams. Budweiser sales should really skyrocket this fall.

PHILADELPHIA

October 2009

IF IT WEREN'T FOR the Dodgers being swept by the Phillies in the National League Championship Series, my sojourn to Philadelphia to cover them would have been sublime. But that "losing the pennant thing" really puts a crimp in your trip.

Philadelphia is the home of Rocky Balboa, Dick Clark, Gogi Grant, Danny Bonaduce (actor, alcoholic), Broderick Crawford (actor, alcoholic), Eddie Fisher (singer, homewrecker), World B. Free, Lola Falana, Betsy Ross, Suzy Kobler, George Jefferson, John Coltrane, Pink, Teller, Fabian, Chaka Fattah, Chubby Checker (who absurdly believes there should be a statue of himself at the Rock n' Roll Hall-of-Fame), Mohini Bhardwaj (no description necessary), funnymen Larry Fine, W.C. Fields, and Richard Gere, two of the most admired women in the world – Grace Kelly and Tina Fey, G Love and Special Sauce, and of course Henry "Box" Brown, an abolitionist who escaped slavery by literally mailing himself to Philadelphia from Richmond, Virginia. (Book rate yet!)

Philadelphia is also one of Hollywood's favorite locations. It's been the setting for *Mannequin, Rocky*, and *The Sixth Sense. The Philadelphia Story* however, was filmed in Hollywood.

The Eagles are still the number one sports team in this town. On Sunday night the Phightin' Phils won 11-0 (and the game wasn't as close as that score would indicate), and most of the coverage in the next day's sports section was "what's wrong with the Eagles?" The Phils are the Rodney Dangerfield of Philadelphia.

Meant to get out to the Mutter Museum, founded originally to educate doctors of the 19th Century and current HMO's. Big attractions include conjoined twins and a catalog of foreign objects removed from bodies. Bring the kids!

The first few nights a Nor'easter blew through town and it was colder than a witch's mooseknuckle. But then the sun came out and temperatures rose from 30 to 70 degrees. It's not always sunny in Philadelphia, but when it is. it's glorious!

I love that the area has regional delicacies – hoagies, soft pretzels, Goldenberg's peanut chews, Tastykakes, and the most famous of all: Philly Cheese Steaks – thinly sliced slippery gristle and melted cheese whiz on a long roll, yet somehow it tastes great. But only in Philadelphia. Everywhere else it's a grease trap on a bun. There is much debate over who serves the best cheese steak, but many locals contend it's Jim's.

And then there's Scrapple. This is a mush of all the pork parts not used elsewhere. Considering what they use in hot dogs, that pretty much leaves the sphincter, doesn't it?

See the Liberty Bell. Yes, it's a real touristy thing to do, but it's worth it.

City statues pay tribute to the three most honored figures in Philadelphia's rich history – Benjamin Franklin, Mike Schmidt, and Sylvester Stallone.

This is the birthplace of two major revolutions – the American and shopping. It is in nearby Westchester that QVC is located, which is why I thought I saw Marie Osmond at baggage claim waiting at the carousel for 42,000 dolls to come down the chute.

Citizens Bank Park, the new home of the Phillies, is a terrific venue, a vast improvement over Veteran's Stadium, which was the world's largest spittoon. Beyond centerfield is the skyline of the city. And in a refreshing change from all the other *new-designed-to-look-like-old* parks, there are actually portions that aren't luxury boxes. It's very fan friendly even though the fans are anything but. Philadelphia fans are tough. Their idea of rally towels is torches and pitchforks. But they're passionate, knowledgeable, and extra intimidating in frigid weather all bundled up in red jackets and hoods. Imagine a Unabomber convention.

And the Phillie Phanatic is the mascot's mascot. He's the Chaplin of big furry blobs.

The Phils also have two terrific announcers: Scott Franzke and Tom McCarthy. But I miss Harry Kalas. Not as much as the fan though, who showed up at one of the games sporting a Mohawk with the initials "HK" cut into one side. Although he could've just been honoring Heidi Klum.

For some reason taxis, and even buses, have the right-of-way over ambulances in the inner City of Brotherly Love.

The Phillies had a great slogan last year: "*Why Can't Us?*"

People say L.A. is weird, but in Sunday night's game the Phightins' former catcher, Darren Daulton, threw out the first pitch. He currently talks to lizards, preaches unconventional theories regarding human existence, and time travels. Even Lauren Conrad from *The Hills* doesn't do that.

In anticipation of the Phillies clinching the pennant, the Philadelphia Municipal Authority greased every pole near the stadium so that rambunctious revilers couldn't climb them. Streetlights, bus signs, even trees were coated with a slippery yellow goo. After how many beers do you ask the question: "Hey, how would a *squirrel* celebrate?"

The charter flight home was long and somber. Arrived back in L.A. at dawn. Yes, it would have been nice to have 20,000 appreciative fans there to greet us but we were more than thrilled just to see the shuttle vans.

Hopefully, next year they'll be greasing the trees around Dodger Stadium.

PHOENIX

March 2010

BACK FROM A SHORT trip to Phoenix to perform some Dodger duties. Having covered spring training in both Arizona and Florida I greatly prefer the *"Valley of the Radio Shack on every corner."* More teams in closer proximity.

The fact that it hailed the first day; that could happen anywhere.

Met up with a few buddies – Howard from LA and Mike & Bob from New York. Middle-aged Jews don't hunt. They go to spring training games and eat less sensibly. Which you pretty much have to since Phoenix is the land of bar food. I don't think there's a place in town that doesn't serve buffalo wings and that includes sushi bars. There are also gift shops in every restaurant. This is very strange to me. But you can enjoy a hearty breakfast at the Cracker Barrel and still pick out that perfect wedding present for sis!

We dined our first night at the Saddle Ranch Chop House. What really sold us was the décor. They had a mechanical bull! Add attractive women and beers from many lands and there's no greater entertainment in the west! "Suburban Cowboy." For middle-aged Jewish guys this was Hooters without the guilt.

Warning: There are freeway cameras that capture you speeding. The fine is a hefty $161.00. I'm told the way to fight it is to claim the person in the photo is not you. Not sure that works in Phoenix. It does in Beverly Hills where most women *do* have different faces than they had two months ago.

Good ribs at Famous Dave's. I know. I've never heard of it either.

On Wednesday I got to announce the Dodger game from their spring Mecca, Camelback Ranch. It was seen on Prime Ticket in southern California and just my luck, nationwide on the MLB network. What a train wreck…and by that I mean mostly *me*. First off, I still have an inflamed cornea so I really just have one good eye. I was fine as long as no one hit the ball to left field. I was counting on watching the monitor but because of the glare of the sun I couldn't see it. They'd be flashing starting line ups on the screen and I'd be merrily talking about something else. Eight years major league experience and viewers must've thought I was there because I'd won an auction.

Then someone batted out of turn. Well, to be more specific – three players batted out of turn. This never happens. Annie said, "How could they screw that up? Isn't baseball like the only thing they do?"

So now I'm on coast-to-coast TV completely confused. Then all the substitutions began and it was like Lucy and Ethel at the candy factory and those chocolates just kept coming down the conveyor belt faster and faster. I may have called a Diamondback pinch runner Diablo Cody, I'm not sure.

Steve Lyons, my partner, said in fourteen years of broadcasting this was the hardest game he's ever had to call. It was surely not my finest hour but still I had a blast. I look forward to doing another game when runners pass each other on the base paths and a meteor lands on the field.

"Happy Hour" has two meanings in Phoenix. The standard one (that I took advantage of, downing six drinks in rapid succession after the game) and also is code for "*Early Bird Specials.*" The old people who aren't filed away in Florida are in the Valley of the Sun. And they love their early dinner specials! So if you stop off at a local eatery looking to wet your whistle and order the "Happy Hour" special, don't be surprised if they bring you boiled chicken.

But, you don't have to be 80 to feel old. Howard and I asked the young desk clerk at the hotel where we might go for a good breakfast (and decorative soaps) and she said at the Westgate shopping mall there was the "Jimmy *Boo-fay.*" What she meant of course was Jimmy Buffet's Margaritaville. Face it, folks; we're *all* "wasting away."

During the flight attendant's safety instructions on my Southwest trip home she warned us that there was no smoking in the lavatories and added, "The fine is $2200. And I'm sure if you were willing to blow that kind of money you would've flown Delta."

Now you may think that all I did in Phoenix was eat, drink, and make a jackass of myself on television. Not true. There was so much more. I rented a car, I hosted Dodger Talk, and I got vigorously patted down. What a jealous boyfriend! I was just taking a picture of her on the mechanical bull.

CINCINNATI/WASHINGTON D.C./ NEW YORK

April 2010

HOME FROM A ROAD trip with the Dodgers that took us to Cincinnati, Washington D.C., and New York. I'm still nursing a swollen cornea, so I had to bring along seven different eye drops. One particular one always had to be refrigerated, so I was forever schlepping a travel mug filled with ice and scrambling to find refrigerators in planes and hotels and clubhouses. I felt like Niles Crane with the sack of flour.

Delta's in-flight magazine a couple of years ago did a puff piece on Cincinnati saying it was *"much like an inland San Francisco."* You'd think the locals would be extremely flattered. No. They were incensed! Why? They thought the magazine was calling them all gay. I hate to tell them, but Cincinnati *is* known as "The Queen City."

It's also the home of Proctor & Gamble. (I wonder if they make Secret deodorant in the same factory as Pringles.) Just as you wouldn't drive a foreign car in Detroit, you better not show up at a Laundromat with a box of Rinso. They'll kill you, wrap you in Bounty, and douse you with Old Spice.

"The Great American Smallpark" was the scene of three "Titanic struggles" as Reds' Hall-of-Fame announcer, Marty Brennaman would say.

Interesting that there's a "Pete Rose Way" leading into the ballpark and yet Pete Rose himself is still banned from baseball. I guess it's the same principle as the Richard Nixon library.

Instead of "hello", the Cincinnati greeting is "Put Pete in the Hall." Same with "goodbye," "I love you," and "this is 911."

Pete was at one of our games. Am I the only one who finds it ironic that one of the Reds' radio sponsors is a casino?

WLW just isn't the same without Gary Burbank. Even his BBQ restaurant closed. One time a food critic disliked his landscaping. And that actually kept people away.

Skyline Chili is to chili what Kate Gosselin is to dancing.

We dropped two out of three to the Reds and flew on to Washington D.C. after Thursday night's tilt. (Tower: "You're clear for takeoff Delta Dodger." Pilot: "Roger that. Goodnight." Tower: "Put Pete in the Hall. Over.")

Stayed at the Ritz-Carlton, Pentagon City. What a gorgeous, elegant hotel. If I were a high level Defense Department official, this is *definitely* where I'd have my nooners.

So much to see in Washington: the monuments, Gennifer Flowers' apartment, Capitol Hill, Paula Jones' apartment, the White House, Monica Lewinsky's apartment, the Smithsonian, the DC Madam's place, the Mint, Elizabeth Ray's apartment, Arlington Cemetery, Donna Rice's apartment, and the Watergate hotel.

Unfortunately, I saw none of those. By the time we got to the hotel it was after 3:00 AM. So I slept. I really wanted to take an hour and wander through the entire Smithsonian but woke up too late. It would be weird to see the set from *MASH* in a museum. I'm sure I would feel a great deal of pride and 150 years old.

The team was given a private showing at the Tourneau watch store in the adjacent mall. Four years ago, these players were buying their jewelry out of the back of station wagons. There was one Rolex I liked. It cost $30,000. True story: I asked the salesman why it was so much and he said it also featured the day and date. I'll stick with my four-dollar gift watch from *AfterMASH*.

The Nationals play in a gleaming new ballpark. A *vast* improvement over RFK stadium, which was the world's largest ashtray.

The press box was high. Like above the timberline. But looking beyond leftfield you can see the Capitol building. If our booth were just a few inches higher we could see the North Pole.

At the park's entrance are statues of Walter Johnson, Josh Gibson, and Frank Howard – three former Washington area ballplayers who went on to become U.S. presidents.

Instead of dot races or giant sausage races, Nationals Park has a presidential race where a goofy oversized Lincoln, Washington, Jefferson, and Teddy Roosevelt waddle and gasp around the warning track. Teddy has never won. Rigging a presidential race – now *that's* a Washington tradition!

We dropped two of three to the struggling Nationals and headed to

Gotham. Instead of flying, the Dodgers chartered a train. That way we didn't have to stop in Trenton. I love train travel. It's great fun to look out the window (with my one good eye) and see places I've never seen before. Who knew there were so many smoke stacks in Wilmington, Delaware? Or that the landfill was so close to Newark?

Stayed at the very swank New York Palace, formerly the Helmsley Palace. The place has lost something without infamous owner Leona Helmsley ("The Queen of Mean") screaming and belittling employees (a practice I assume she continued in Federal Prison, while serving time for income tax evasion. "Why aren't there fresh flowers in this exercise yard?!" "You call that a rape?!")

The rain we had been ducking in Cincinnati and DC caught up with us in New York. Monday night's game with the Mets was washed out and we played a doubleheader on Tuesday night. Oh, was *that* fun! Seven hours of baseball in 37 degree weather with 40 mile-per-hour gusts, and we lost both games. But if you can believe *The New York Times*, this was *still* preferable to sitting through the new revival of *Promises Promises*.

Best hamburger in New York is at Citi Field. Join the others in line at the Shake Shack.

Yankee Stadium, the REAL Yankee Stadium, is now just a pile of rubble. Who needs tradition and cherished memories when you can have luxury suites?

Donald Trump is speaking at the Learning Annex. I think the topic is "*How to communicate with your departed pets.*" What everyone assumes is his hair is really his former dog, Rex.

The final game of the road trip was held in a typhoon and the Mets won that one, too. There were so many hot dog wrappers blown onto the field, you'd think it was a ticker tape parade down Fifth Avenue for astronauts. The Dodgers staggered back home after going 2-7. Was it the pitching? Hitting? Poor defense? Skipper Joe Torre had another theory. He turned to me on the plane and said, "YOU!" I answered, "Hey, I'm playing with one eye. You're lucky we won two!"

BOSTON

June 2010

THIS YEAR FOR INTERLEAGUE play, the Dodgers headed to Boston to take on the Red Sox. It wasn't as highly anticipated as the big Kansas City-Pittsburgh grudge match but still there was some nominal interest. Enough, that I made the trip.

There was lots of intrigue – it was the first time the once-beloved Bosox, Manny Ramirez, had returned since quitting on the team and forcing them to trade him in 2008. And it was the first return of Joe Torre, the former Yankees skipper. Plus, the night before, the Lakers defeated the Celtics to win the NBA Finals. Here's how much New Englanders hated us: Red Sox fans were chanting "Beat L.A.! Beat L.A.!" earlier in the week, when the Sox were playing the Arizona Diamondbacks.

Personally, I had the added treat of meeting up with Matt for the Father's Day Weekend. How often can a father and son share a love for the game and root against each other?

The Boston weather was absolutely glorious the first two days. 80 degrees, sunny, no snow. By day three there was 1000% humidity and ferocious thunderstorms, but that still didn't deter 37,430 Red Sox faithful from coming out and being Fenway's 591st straight sellout. That's impressive, especially since their promotion was "Life Threatening Lightening Night."

When the weather is nice, Boston is a sensational walking city, which was very fortuitous since the two-mile trip from my hotel to Fenway Park was $30 by cab.

The reaction to Manny for his first at bat was mostly cheers. However, as the night wore on, the more booze; the more boos. Had the game gone extra innings, by the 12th they would have booed Nelson Mandela.

And when all these plastered tosspots get in their cars and pull onto the highway there's a gigantic sign right at the entrance imploring them to buy guns. The billboard is actually a joke, but when you're totally shit-faced I imagine the irony is somewhat lost on you.

My hotel was the Inter-Continental. It was quite lovely with first-class accommodations, but I don't think I'll stay there again. Way too far to walk to the nearest Dunkin' Donuts. At least two blocks, or $12 by cab.

Yes, I have pedestrian tastes, but I prefer Dunkin' Donuts to Finagle-a-Bagel.

The wildly popular Duck tours originated here. Boston is the only city where the majority of its buses float.

I passed by the *"Cheers"* bar several times and I always get a little choked up. I couldn't help thinking, "Wow, they've made a lot of money off me."

On Saturday my son and I took a tour inside the Green Monster (that large wall in leftfield Fenway Park). It was like stepping into a scene from *Papillon*. A dank dark passageway with the back of the metal scoreboard on one side and antiquated concrete walls and pillars on the other. Two guys operate the lowest tech scoreboard since the Christians & the lions. They slide aluminum panels through slots. Amazingly, these two guys haven't come out from inside that scoreboard since 1995. Leftfielders bring them food. Visitors are invited to sign the wall. All the greats from the game of baseball have lent their signatures. I signed right below Rachel Maddow.

After the tilt, Dodger owner Frank McCourt threw a fabulous party for the staff, players, and crashing Dodger Talk hosts. I mean, there I was, hob knobbing with Vin Scully. I just wish I wasn't holding that stupid blue drink in the Cosmo glass at the time. Even Manny attended. Of course he would show up at an execution if there was free food.

I brought some of the little pizzas they were serving to the scoreboard guys the next day. They were very excited and were going to store them for winter.

Father's Day brunch was a delightful affair out in suburban Natick, home of New England's biggest mall and Doug Flutie. Met Matt's future in-laws and managed not to horrify them. Natick was so lush and green. I imagined it in the autumn with all the leaves turning vivid reds, golds. oranges, and witches being torched outside the Whole Foods Market.

The team charter flight left Boston at 1:30 in the morning following our third straight loss Sunday night. But we were first in line to take off, the pilot proudly announced. Yeah, well, who else has flights leaving at 1:30 Monday morning? It was a long flight – six-and-a-half hours. Fortunately they showed a couple of episodes of *The Good Wife,* and that kept the players enthralled. I couldn't sleep. The "Flintstones Ambien" had no effect. I finally staggered home at 6:00 AM; 9:00 body time.

It was a memorable Father's Day trip. The only thing that could have made it better was if (a) I was with both my kids (Annie is so sweet: she bought me the latest *National Examiner* with the headline demanding they re-open the Natalie Wood case now!), (b) I didn't get drenched in a thunderstorm that heralded in the beginning of summer and Armageddon, and (c) the Dodgers had won even one of the three games. My road record is now 2-12. I think my next Dodger road trip will be to Cambodia.

NEW YORK

November 2010

WENT TO NEW YORK for Thanksgiving this year. There's something really special about watching the Macy's Day Parade on television when you're actually *in* the city.

The flight to New York was a cross between the Beverly Hills Gymboree and *Lord of the Flies*. If the flight attendants went down the aisle selling noise-canceling ear buds, people would have paid a thousand dollars for them.

We arrived at 4:05. Winter arrived at 4:11.

Rented a nice apartment on the Upper East Side. Among the conditions in the contract – we were not allowed to invite Charlie Sheen over.

Somebody on the street was distributing free Kabbalah shopping bags. The wisdom of the ages and a way to carry your liquor!

The giant Christmas tree was up in Rockefeller Center. A bit of a letdown. But I'm sure it looks better at night when the scaffolding is all lit up.

Heath Ledger's apartment is for sale. $5,000,000 but includes ghost.

Thanksgiving morning. Threatening skies, 39 degrees, and windy. I joke, but if you're ever in New York, at least once in your life, do treat yourself and see the Macy's Day Parade in HD.

Some highlights from this year's march-past:

- Al Roker interviewing Ben Rappaport, the star of NBC's uh, "hit" new show, *Outsourced*, and calling him "a fish out of comedy."
- Offstage announcer: "Coming up next: a one-of-a-kind performance from the U.S. Pizza Twirling Team!"
- The cheerleading captains all-star squad. Can you imagine the bitch quotient there? From daughter, Annie: "A thousand girls all yelling, "*I* want to be in front!"
- The Mickey Mouse balloon doing a "Heil Hitler" salute. I don't

think you'd see that if Eisner and Katzenberg were still running Disney.

- The Black Eyed Peas medley from some high school marching band. I never really appreciated their music until I heard it with tubas.
- The kids dressed as dancing sausages on the Jimmy Dean float.
- Jessica Simpson, who's gained a pound or two, appropriately riding the Pillsbury Doughboy float.
- Offstage announcer: "Coming up next: the official start of the holiday season with Joan Rivers!"

I dunno. The parade is just not the same anymore without the Bullwinkle, Underdog, and Nathan Lane balloons.

The real reason to be in New York for Thanksgiving:*The Odd Couple* marathon on WPIX.

There's a lot of daring theater on Broadway currently. The risk-taking *Elf* musical, the untested *Lion King*, the chancy *Mary Poppins*, the groundbreaking *Pee Wee Herman Show*, not to mention, the always controversial *Donny & Marie Show*.

The long-delayed *Spiderman* rock musical is due to finally go into previews. Considering all the accidents they've already had, it's more like a rock musical of *The Hurt Locker*.

Your best theater bet is *La Bete* starring David Hyde Pierce and Mark Rylance. David was kind enough to stop the stage manager from running us off after the show.

Lots of *Frasier* alums on Broadway these days. Kelsey Grammer in *La Cage Aux Folles*, Bebe Neuwirth in *the Addams Family*, and Eddie has gone into *Driving Miss Daisy*. Thanks again, David, for a wonderful evening.

Remember when stores opened at 5:00 AM on Black Friday? Kohl's opened at 3:00, thus getting a big jump on all those homeless shoppers.

There's now a dress code for New York City taxi drivers. No more tank tops. No more bathing suits. They are still allowed to reek, though. They'd quit en masse if they couldn't do *that*.

Little Night Music was a huge disappointment. What should be a light frothy soufflé, in the hands of director Trevor Nunn, is a leaden German pancake. But Bernadette Peters sang "Send in the Clowns" beautifully, and Elaine Stritch remembered many of her lines.

A man reading Sondheim's bio in the row behind me said to his wife: "I didn't know that – he also did the music for *Company*." Probably a Tony voter.

Don Draper would be proud. This is Cadillac's new holiday slogan: "This year, give the gift of asphalt."

Came home on Saturday rather than Sunday for the same reason I don't go to Macy's at 5:00 AM on Black Friday.

Managed to negotiate JFK without getting X-Rayed. And that's with Kabbalah bags. Personally, I'm outraged by these new, highly invasive, demeaning screening methods. Either preserve our constitutional rights and discontinue them, or let women pat down the men.

Now that Joan Rivers has given the okay, the holiday season is officially here. Have a fabulous one!

HAWAII

December 2010

WE LIKE TO THINK of it as our second home. Our two-bedroom condo in the E-Coli Village in Wailea, Maui. Okay, we don't own it, and if we show up any other time than the three weeks we have it booked we'll be shot on sight, but still, it's ours alone.

Hawaii is my sanctuary, my oasis. The beauty and serenity are unmatched, and as dismal as the state of the world is, somehow it's not nearly as bleak when reported by newscasters in Aloha shirts. Once again the Levine family ventured to the land where the volcanoes meet the cabanas.

There's no better way to relax on Maui the first night than by learning you might have Hepatitis A. I came across a story online warning anybody who ordered a sandwich at Jerry's Deli in Westwood on specific days that they were in danger of contracting this acute infectious disease. Apparently, the nimrod who made the sandwiches was infected and possibly passed it along. (As if the chopped liver sandwiches *alone* couldn't kill ya.) My wife was one of the unlucky sandwich orderers. Customers were urged to get a Hepatitis A vaccine or a Gamma Globulin shot in the next two days. Good luck on Maui.

Remember the nurse's office in your elementary school? She had some band-aids and a bottle of baby aspirin. Well that's the equivalent of a full-service Maui hospital. Debby called around for Gamma Globulin or a vaccine. She might as well have been asking for Plutonium. The clinics were all in shopping malls. One doctor's office address was an apartment number.

We finally found a place next to a nail salon. Debby got the shot. It cost $350, and Jerry's is refusing to reimburse because they "didn't know the employee had Hepatitis at the time so they're not liable." Oh really??? I don't think it will require Erin Brockovich to win *that* case in court.

The latest Twitter trend is to Tweet where you are every five seconds. So for those who don't follow me on Twitter, here are some entries:

@Maui airport – waiting for shuttle van to Alamo Rental Cars. 1:40 PM

@Maui airport – still waiting for shuttle van. 2:40 PM

@Alamo – waiting in long line to get my car. 3:30 PM

@Alamo – Finally get the keys. 4:05 PM

@ Alamo – In car. Chasing Alamo employees around the lot, trying to run them down. Sure, NOW they move fast. 4:10 PM

Forget the Alamo. They're the Goldman Sachs of rental car companies.

How to get a better table at Mama's Fish House: Have the hostess spill a glass of water on your wife. Better table, free t-shirt, and round of drinks! Too bad it wasn't wine. Those appetizers looked really yummy!

There's a "backpack bandit" who has robbed four local banks at gunpoint. *Four?* Where the fuck is HAWAII 5-0? What are you idiots doing? Stop trading barbs and joy riding in your product-placement Chevy and protect us for godsakes! Jack Lord is spinning in either his grave or wax museum; I forget where he is now.

Obama isn't even popular in Hawaii anymore.

There's more Reggae music being played in Hawaii than Hawaiian music. To save face they call it "Jawaiian." And the closer we got to the holidays the more we heard "Chriswaiian" music.

Two sure signs that the world is coming to an end: The Roy's in Kihei is being replaced by a Ruby Tuesday's. And a tour bus was spotted at the Kahului Walmart.

At one point we had Matt, his fiancée Kim, and Annie joining us at the same time. Five people, all trying to recharge their Kindles, eReaders, iPads, iPods, iPhones, laptops, and cameras at once – there were not enough outlets. My wife and I had to move out to the Grand Wailea.

Now that Hilton owns the Grand Wailea, they're cutting corners and foolishly assuming guests don't notice. They recently eliminated all mini-bars and fired the twenty long-time employees who serviced them. I guess the twelve dollars profit on every Toblerone bar just wasn't enough for them.

We were given a gorgeous room overlooking the parking lot, a septic tank, and the back end of another hotel… excuse me, I mean, a "mountain view." You say, "How did we get so lucky?" We're Hilton

Honors members!

Our room safe didn't work so we called Security. They said they'd send someone up in five minutes. It took twenty. Now, it's one thing if Room Service is a little tardy but Security? And it's not like we can call the Hawaii 5-0 guys. They're still investigating Pearl Harbor (although I understand they almost have a suspect).

Grand Wailea security officers must all be former Alamo customer representatives.

Actual Hawaiian headline: *Kids Smoke Nutmeg For Cheap High.* Hey, gasoline costs $3.95 a gallon. Pretty soon stoners won't even be able to afford spices.

Black Friday sale at the shops at the Kapalua Ritz-Carlton!! Mark Ups slashed to only 60%!!!

Here's the kind of shit you do in Hawaii: watch giant sea turtles bob in the water on the beach. For twenty minutes. Hey, don't laugh. It was still far more entertaining than the NBC Fall line-up.

Some nights we had meteor showers. I wonder how many tourists waited around for rainbows.

Went to Mama's Fish House again. Told Debby that if they gave us a bad table she had to "take one for the team." The problem was finding a nice evening dress that's also water-resistant.

Nothing deters my love for Hawaii, even the two minor earthquakes we experienced. But that was just the islands' way of saying, "Don't be homesick."

When there's a big earthquake (and it's highly unlikely – there's only one active volcano in the area), you do have eight full minutes to get to higher ground before the tsunami hits. On the other hand, Hawaii papayas are really sweet!

The Honolulu Marathon was held again. 25.000 runners all yelling, "On your left!" I did not participate this year because a) I wasn't in Honolulu, b) I'm not from Kenya, and c) unlike the other Hollywood types on the isles, I don't have a housekeeper or nanny to run for me.

Most of the wet weather we got came during our last few days. I thought it was the influx of tourists that angered *Hina Kuluua*, the Hawaiian Mistress of Rain. Wrong. She just found out that Rain is not going to leave his wife for her.

Cell phone service was also out for a day. I guess, *Wendy Williams,* the Goddess of Incessant Talking, was also out of sorts.

Flew home on the redeye. Usually I never fly First Class unless a network or studio is paying for it. So I haven't flown First Class in years. But Debby and I decided to use miles and upgrade, hoping to maybe get some sleep.

We boarded first and sat patiently as the coach passengers filed past us to their seats. Now this I've never experienced before – random people just taking shots at us. "Oooh, it's the *First Class* people." "Look who the *lucky* ones are." "Got enough room in those seats?" What the hell?!

Since when did travelers turn hostile towards First Class passengers? And this was in Maui after a vacation. What happens in Detroit? Does the guy from 42A just enter the plane and arbitrarily slug the man in 3B?

By the way, the seats weren't that big, there were no footrests, the meal was a cold cup of corn chowder with six grapes, and we didn't sleep. Is it really worth staging another Russian Revolution over American Airlines' supposed premiere service?

So now we're home, just in time for the holidays and monsoons. Verbal abuse and earthquakes aside, we had a fabulous time. Oh sure, my wife's skin is a little red, but hey, at least it's not yellow.

Mele Kalikimaka me ka Hau'oli Makahiki Hou. (Merry Christmas and pass the nutmeg)

ABOUT THE AUTHOR

KEN LEVINE IS AN Emmy winning writer /director/ producer/ major league baseball announcer. In a career that has spanned over 30 years Ken has worked on *MASH, Cheers, Frasier, The Simpsons, Wings, Everybody Loves Raymond, Becker, Dharma & Greg,* and has co-created his own series including *Almost Perfect* starring Nancy Travis. He and his partner wrote the feature *Volunteers.*

Ken has also been the radio/TV play-by-play voice of the Baltimore Orioles, Seattle Mariners, and San Diego Padres, and has hosted pre-and-postgame shows for the Los Angeles Dodgers.

A book about his year in Baltimore w published by Villard in 1993 entitled *It's Gone...No, Wait A Minute.*

In 2011 Ken returned to the Seattle Mariners where he again does play-by-play. He currently contributes to the Huffington Post, has his own very popular blog, byKenLevine.com, and later this year will release his third book, *The Me Generation...by Me,* a first person account of growing up in the turbulent '60s.

Made in the USA
Lexington, KY
15 March 2011